▲ Classical guitar:

Traditionally associated with Spanish and classical music, this guitar is also used in folk and country.

The nylon strings (formerly gut) are set wider than on a steel-string guitar to enable the right-hand fingers to pick accurately.

The combination of smaller body and thicker, softer strings gives the classical guitar a mellower tone.

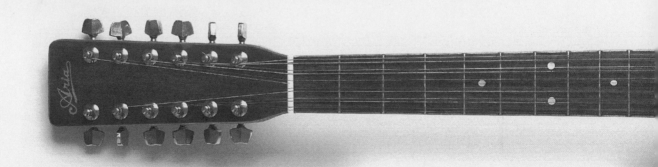

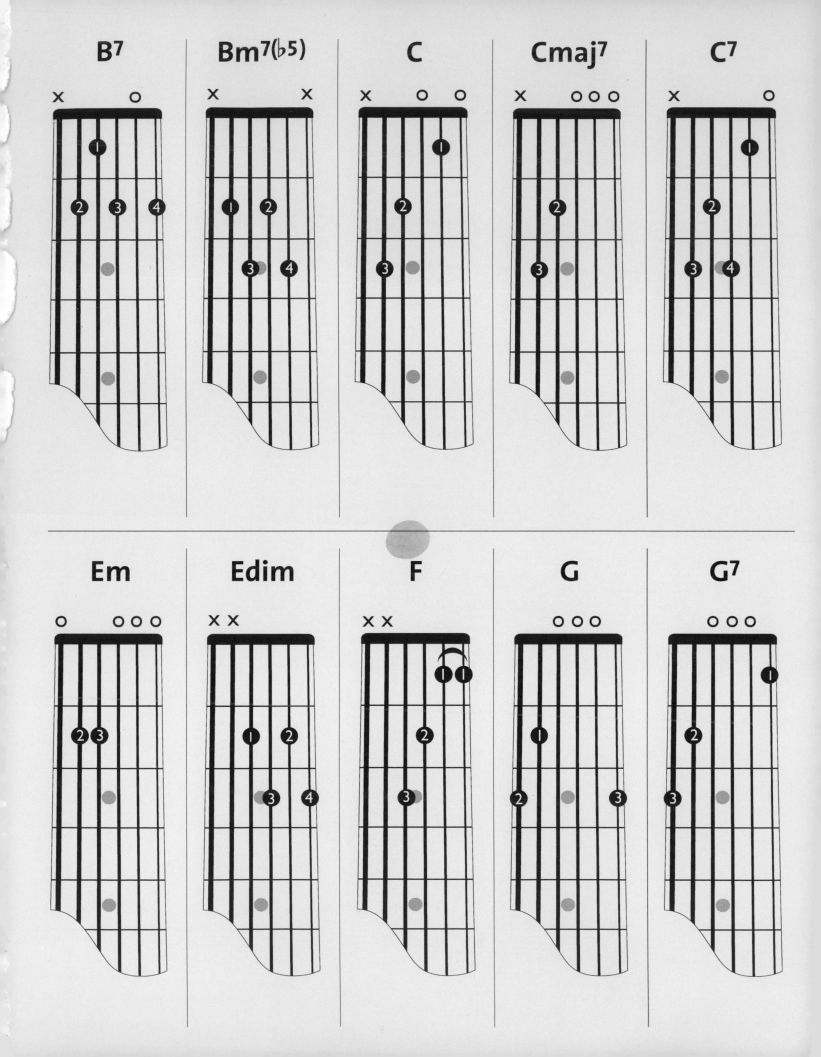

A New Tune A Day *for* Acoustic Guitar
Pull-out Chord Chart

▼ Twelve-string acoustic:

Essentially identical to a standard Western guitar except for the inclusion of an extra six strings.

The twelve strings are arranged in pairs, or courses, in a manner reminiscent of the lute: the bottom four standard E, A, D and G strings are each coupled with a string an octave higher, while the top two B and E strings each have an identical twin. The result is a very full, somewhat jangly tone.

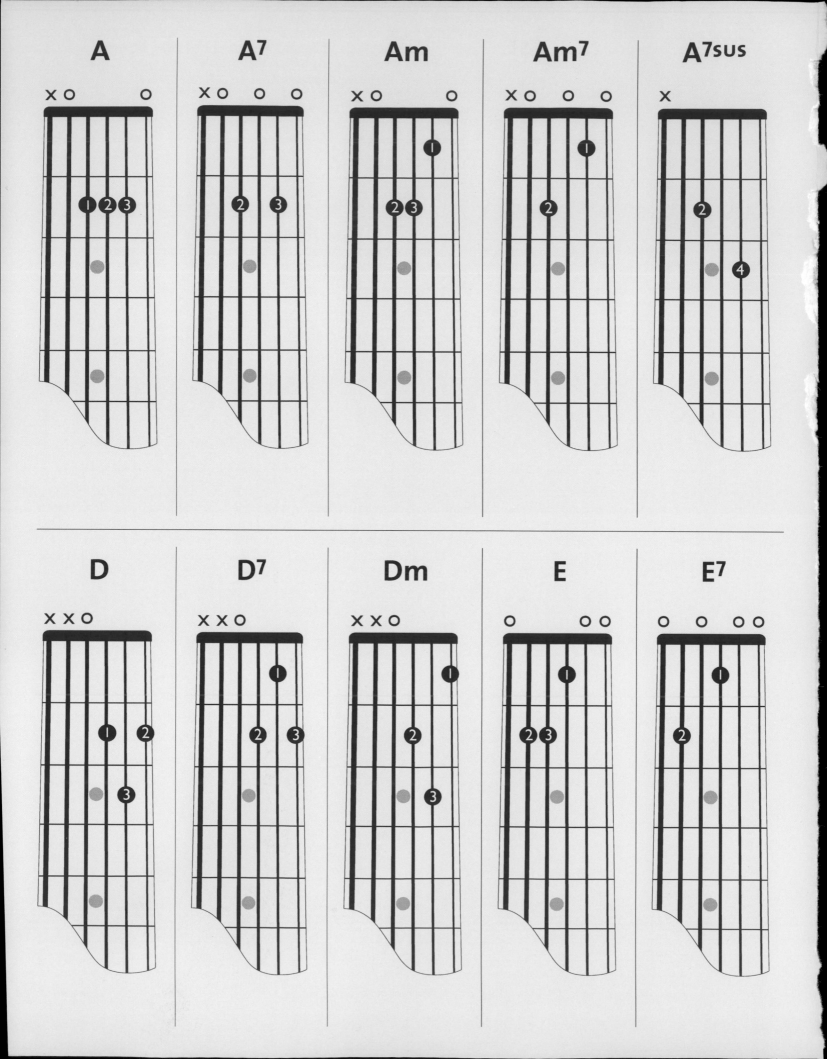

A New Tune A Day™
for Acoustic Guitar

Boston Music Company
part of the Music Sales Group
New York/Los Angeles/Nashville/London/Berlin/Copenhagen/Madrid/Paris/Sydney/Tokyo

Foreword

Since its appearance in the early 1930s, C. Paul Herfurth's original *A Tune A Day* series has become the most popular instrumental teaching method of all time. Countless music students have been set on their path by the clear, familiar, proven material, and the logical, sensibly-paced progression through the lessons within the book.

The teacher will find that the new books have been meticulously rewritten by experienced teachers: instrumental techniques and practices have been updated and the musical content has been completely overhauled.

The student will find clearly presented, uncluttered material, with familiar tunes and a gentle introduction to the theoretical aspects of music. The books are now accompanied by audio CDs of examples and backing tracks to help the student develop a sense of rhythm, intonation and performance at an early stage.

As in the original books, tests are given following every five lessons. Teachers are encouraged to present these as an opportunity to ensure that the student has a good overview of the information studied up to this point.

The following extract from the foreword to the original edition remains as true today as the day it was written:

The value of learning to count aloud from the very beginning cannot be over-estimated. Only in this way can a pupil sense rhythm. Rhythm, one of the most essential elements of music, and usually conspicuous by its absence in amateur ensemble playing, is emphasized throughout.

Eventual success in mastering the instrument depends on regular and careful application to its technical demands. Daily practice should not extend beyond the limits of the player's physical endurance — the aim should be the gradual development of tone control alongside assured finger-work.

Music-making is a lifelong pleasure, and at its heart is a solid understanding of the principles of sound production and music theory. These books are designed to accompany the student on these crucial first steps: the rewards for study and practice are immediate and lasting.

Welcome to the world of music!

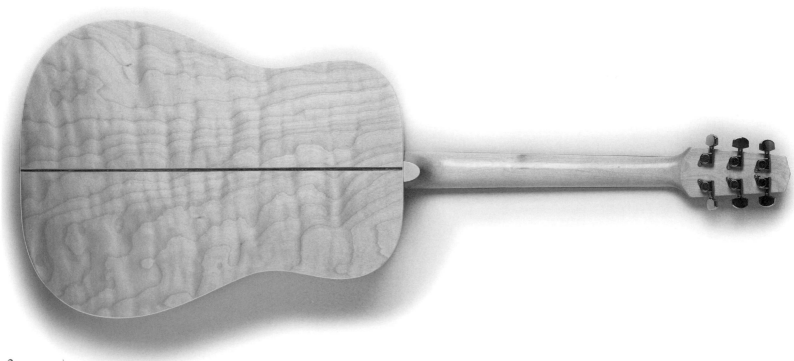

Published by
Boston Music Company

Exclusive Distributors:
Music Sales Corporation
180 MADISON AVENUE, 24TH FLOOR, NEW YORK NY10016, USA.
Music Sales Limited
DISTRIBUTION CENTRE, NEWMARKET ROAD, BURY ST EDMUNDS, SUFFOLK IP33 3YB, UK.
Music Sales Pty Limited
UNITS 3-4, 17 WILLFOX ST, CONDELL PARK, NSW, 2200 AUSTRALIA

This book © Copyright 2006 Boston Music Company,
A Division of Music Sales Corporation, New York

Edited by David Harrison
Music processed by Paul Ewers Music Design
Original compositions and arrangements by John Blackwell
Cover and book designed by Chloë Alexander
Photography by Matthew Ward
Model: Martin Hadley
Printed in the EU
Backing tracks by Guy Dagul
CD performance by John Blackwell and David Harrison
CD recorded, mixed and mastered by Jonas Persson and John Rose

Sincere thanks to the City Literary Institute, London, for their
invaluable help.

Your Guarantee of Quality
As publishers, we strive to produce every book to the highest commercial
standards. The music has been freshly engraved and the book has been
carefully designed to minimize awkward page turns and to make playing
from it a real pleasure. Throughout, the printing and binding have been
planned to ensure a sturdy, attractive publication which should give years
of enjoyment. If your copy fails to meet our high standards, please inform
us and we will gladly replace it.

www.musicsales.com

Contents

Rudiments of music

The staff

Music is written on a grid of five lines called a *staff*.

At the beginning of each staff is placed a special symbol called a *clef* to describe the approximate range of the instrument for which the music is written.

This example shows a *treble clef*, generally used for melody instruments.

The staff is divided into equal sections of time, called *bars* or *measures*, by *barlines*.

Note values

Different symbols are used to show the time value of *notes*, and each *note value* has an equivalent symbol for a rest, representing silence.

The **eighth note**, often used to signify a half beat, is written with a solid head and a stem with a tail. The eighth-note rest is also shown.

The **quarter note**, often used to signify one beat, is written with a solid head and a stem. The quarter-note rest is also shown.

The **half note** is worth two quarter notes. It is written with a hollow head and a stem. The half-note rest is placed on the middle line.

The **whole note** is worth two half notes. It is written with a hollow head. The whole-note rest hangs from the fourth line.

Other note values

Note values can be increased by half by adding a dot after the notehead. Here a half note and a quarter note are together worth a *dotted* half note.

Grouping eighth notes

Where two or more eighth notes follow each other, they can be joined by a *beam* from stem to stem.

Time signatures

The number of beats in a bar is determined by the *time signature*, a pair of numbers placed after the clef.
The upper number shows how many beats each bar contains, while the lower number indicates what kind of note value
is used to represent a single beat. This lower number is a fraction of a whole note, so that 4 represents quarter notes
and 8 represents eighth notes.

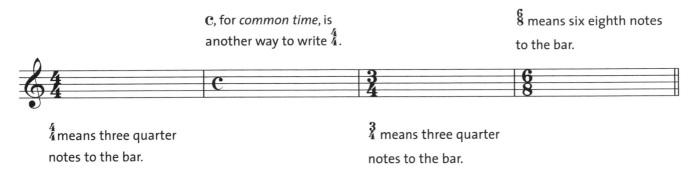

C, for *common time*, is another way to write $\frac{4}{4}$.

$\frac{6}{8}$ means six eighth notes to the bar.

$\frac{4}{4}$ means three quarter notes to the bar.

$\frac{3}{4}$ means three quarter notes to the bar.

Note names

Notes are named after the first seven letters of the alphabet and are written on lines or spaces on the staff,
according to pitch.

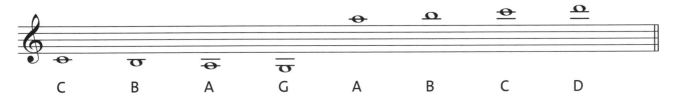

Accidentals

The pitch of a note can be altered up or down a *semitone* by the use of sharp and flat symbols.
These temporary pitch changes are known as *accidentals*.

The *sharp* (♯) raises the pitch of a note.

The *natural* (♮) returns the note to its original pitch.

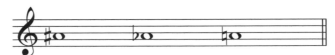

The *flat* (♭) lowers the pitch of a note.

Ledger lines

Ledger lines are used to extend the range of the staff for low or high notes.

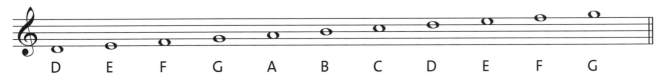

Barlines

Various different types of barlines are used:

Double barlines divide one section of music from another.

Final barlines show the end of a piece of music.

Repeat signs show a section to be repeated.

Before you play:

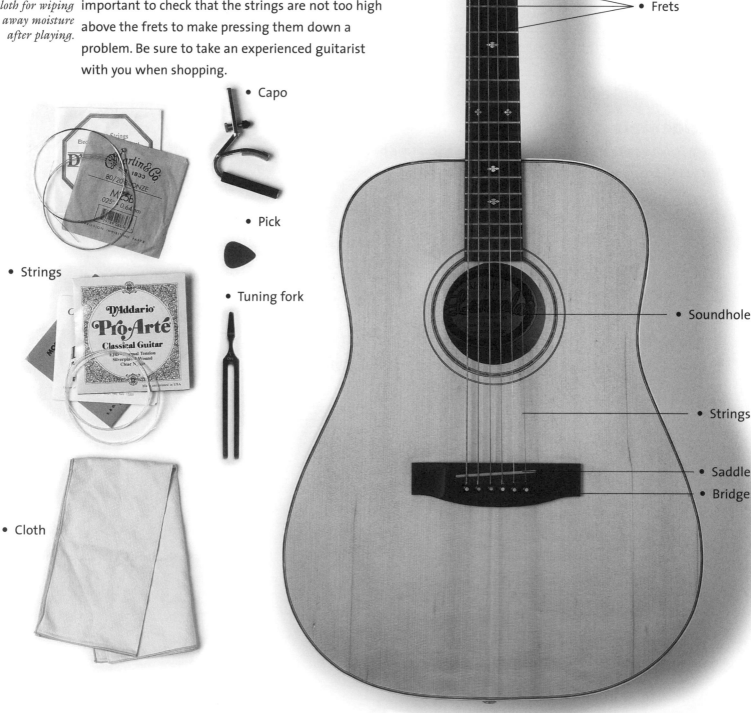

Which guitar?

The standard acoustic, or "Western" style guitar, has steel strings. Be sure the body of the guitar is not too big for the player to comfortably reach the strings with the right hand.

Always keep a spare set of strings in the case, and a cloth for wiping away moisture after playing.

Classical or Western style guitars are equally suitable for the beginner, and they are tuned in exactly the same way. The Classical guitar will have a wider neck, which suits students with larger hands, and—with nylon strings—makes left-hand technique a little less strenuous. The Western style guitar has steel strings (these are harder to press onto the frets) and tend to have larger bodies, but are the instrument of choice for the traditional folk, rock and country sound. If choosing steel, it is important to check that the strings are not too high above the frets to make pressing them down a problem. Be sure to take an experienced guitarist with you when shopping.

- Tuning pegs
- Nut
- Neck
- Frets
- Capo
- Pick
- Strings
- Tuning fork
- Soundhole
- Strings
- Saddle
- Bridge
- Cloth

Care of the guitar

If your guitar comes with a hardshell case, then this is the best place to store it. If you carry your guitar with you, you might want to invest in a lighter, soft gig bag. As with any wooden instrument, the guitar is very susceptible to temperature and humidity. Be sure to keep your guitar away from radiators, sunlight, and moisture.

Accessories

A tuning fork is useful, and an electronic guitar tuner may be an asset if tuning is a challenge. A set of thin, medium, and heavy picks may also be useful when strumming for an extended period. A music stand will greatly improve your practice comfort.

Basic posture

When playing, sit on a chair that allows you to sit quite upright. A dining chair is usually best, although taller players may need a higher seat. In any case the chair should allow the feet to sit squarely on the floor with the knees at right angles. The guitar should feel supported and not likely to fall forward. Some students will like to rest the guitar on crossed legs, right over left.

Lesson 1

goals:

1. **Recognize note values**
2. **Learn string names**
3. **Count the pulse while playing**

For left-handed students: Unlike most instruments, the guitar can be completely reversed for left-handers. It is possible to restring the guitar in the opposite order, and read all the diagrams accordingly. If you are struggling to play the conventional way, you might like to consider this option.

Play the strings either with the thumb or fingers of the right hand, in a gentle plucking motion. The hand should stay relaxed: aim for an easy, fluid stroke.

The six open strings

The strings on the guitar are all named after different letters of the alphabet. Notice how the two outer strings are both called **E** (more about this in later lessons).

Right-hand technique

Play the notes in this lesson with the thumb or fingertip, whichever is more comfortable.

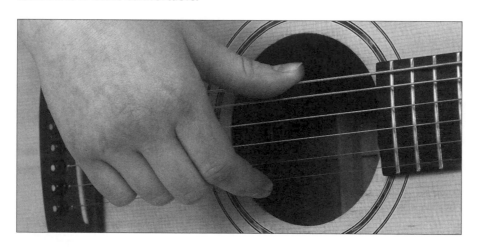

E A D G B E

Count out loud as you play the following exercises.

Exercise 1:

Whole notes last for four beats. Pluck the string and let it ring while steadily counting 1, 2, 3, 4. The sound should begin with the first count and last until the end of each bar.

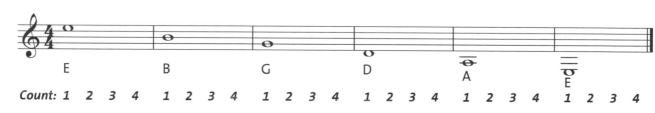

E   B   G   D   A   E

Count: 1 2 3 4   1 2 3 4   1 2 3 4   1 2 3 4   1 2 3 4   1 2 3 4

Exercise 2:

Half notes last for two beats each. Play the first note in each bar with a count of 1, 2 before playing the next note with a count of 3, 4.

E   B   G   D   A   E

Count: 1 2 3 4   1 2 3 4   1 2 3 4   1 2 3 4   1 2 3 4   1 2 3 4

Exercise 3:

Quarter notes last for one beat. You should be playing one note for each of the counts 1, 2, 3, 4.

E   B   G   D   A   E

Count: 1 2 3 4   1 2 3 4   1 2 3 4   1 2 3 4   1 2 3 4   1 2 3 4

Pieces for Lesson 1

Chimes

Blackwell

E   G   B   D   G

All Through The Night

Welsh Lullaby

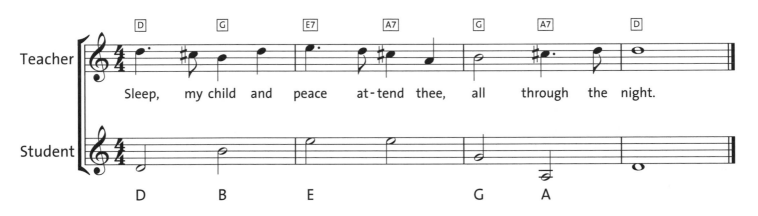

Teacher — Sleep, my child and peace at-tend thee, all through the night.

Student — D   B   E   G   A

Ode To Joy (theme from 9th Symphony)

Beethoven

1. **Left-hand position**
2. **First and second string note names**
3. **New notes on the staff**
4. **Quarter-note rest**

The fingers of the left hand are numbered, from 1 to 4, according to the picture below.

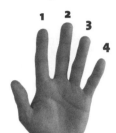

Left-hand position

Aim for a clear sound without buzzing when the string is picked, and bring the fingertip onto the fretboard as close to right angles as possible.

New notes

F

Left-hand finger 1 on fret 1, 1st string

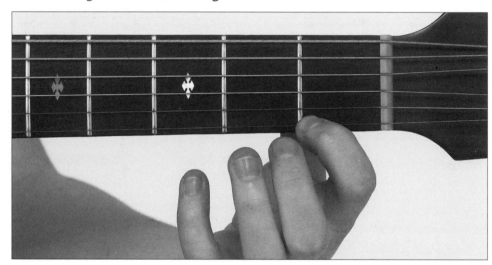

G

Left-hand finger 3 on fret 3, 1st string

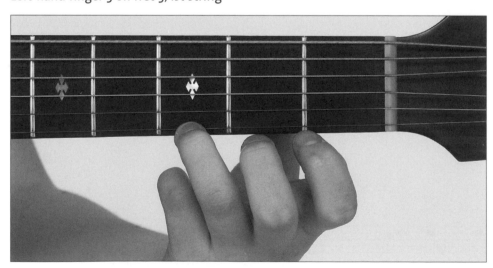

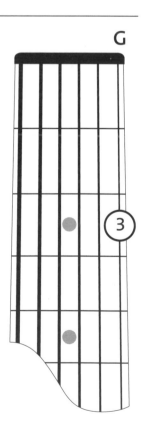

C

Left-hand finger 1 on fret 1, 2nd string

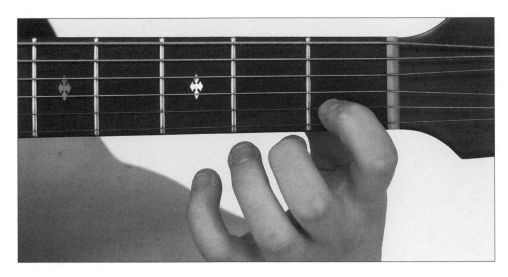

C

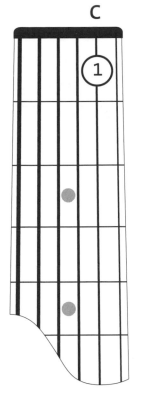

A comfortable left-hand position is essential. Let the thumb rest gently on the back of the neck (see lesson 4) and bring the fingers onto the fretboard at right angles to the strings, close to the fret.

D

Left-hand finger 3 on fret 3, 2nd string

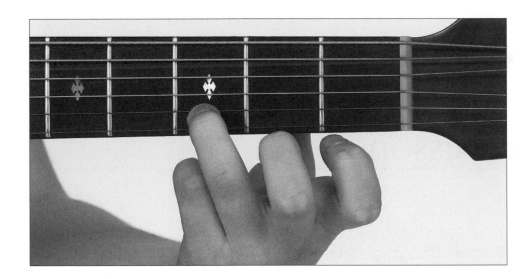

D

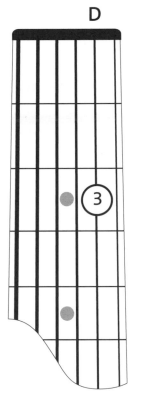

Exercise 1:

In this exercise the notes F and E are played. Be sure to count the note values. In the fourth bar, you will see two quarter-note rests: 𝄽. Count 1 beat for each of the quarter notes and their rests, but do not play any sound when you see the rests.

F   E   F   E   F   E   F

Count: 1   2   3   4   1   2   3   4   1   2   3   4   1   2   3   4   1   2   3   4

Exercise 2:

You will play the note G with your 3rd (ring) finger. The other note is an open string you learned in lesson 1.

Count: 1 2 3 4   1 2 3 4   1 2 3 4   1 2 3 4   1 2 3 4

Exercise 3:

Pressing down the 2nd string on the 1st fret will give you a C note.

Count: 1 2 3 4   1 2 3 4   1 2 3 4   1 2 3 4   1 2 3 4

Exercise 4:

Pressing down on the 3rd fret on string 2 will give you a D note. Use your 3rd (ring) finger.

Count: 1 2 3 4   1 2 3 4   1 2 3 4   1 2 3 4   1 2 3 4

Fingering numbers

In these pieces you will have to remember the positions of the notes on the fretboard.

The small numbers next to the notes are the finger numbers. For now, they will be the same as the fret numbers in each case. A **zero** indicates that the string is played **open**.

Pieces for Lesson 2

Jingle Bells

Traditional

Jin - gle bells,   jin - gle bells,   jin - gle all the way.   Oh what fun it   is to ride a

one horse o - pen sleigh hey!   Jin - gle bells,   jin - gle bells,   jin - gle all the

way.   Oh what fun it   is to ride a   one horse o - pen sleigh.

Pieces for Lesson 2

Skip To My Lou

American Folk Song

Be my part - ner skip my Lou, be my part - ner skip my Lou.

Be my part - ner skip my Lou, be my part - ner dar - ling.

Au Clair de la Lune

French Folk Song

Au clair de la lu - ne, mon a - mi Pier - rot.

Prê - te moi ta plu - me pour éc - rire un mot.

Ode To Joy (theme from 9th Symphony)

Beethoven

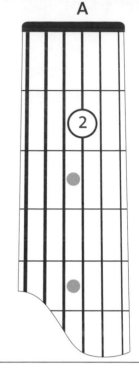

goals:

1. **Two-note chords**
2. **A on the 3rd string**
3. **Picking technique**

4. **Dotted half notes**
5. **$\frac{3}{4}$ time signature**

New notes
A

Left-hand finger 2 on 2nd fret, 3rd string

Be sure not to touch the strings on either side of the 3rd string, and aim for a smoothly curved middle finger that comes down as near as possible at right angles to the fingerboard.

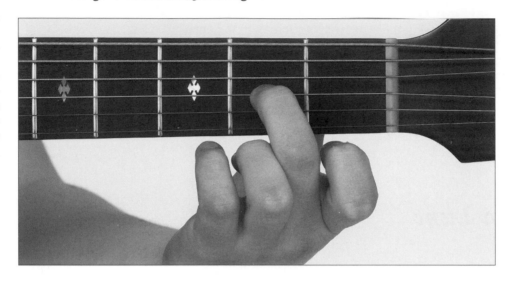

Exercise 1:

Play the A note on the 3rd string, using your left-hand 2nd (middle) finger, and the G note learned in lesson 1.

Dotted half notes

A dot beside a note adds half the length of the note: $\textcolor{black}{\textsf{♩. = ♩ + ♪}}$

Exercise 2: Theme from *Peer Gynt*

Grieg

Notice the new time signature—$\frac{3}{4}$.

Each bar has three quarter notes. Look at the dotted half note in bar 8: this lasts for three beats—a whole bar.

The next four exercises introduce common combinations of notes on the top three strings.

Exercise 3:

Play the C and E together: fret C on the B string and play it together with the E (open 1st string).
They should both sound clearly without any damping or muffling of the strings.

Exercise 4:

Now try G and D together.

This time make sure that the finger fretting the D doesn't interfere with the open 3rd string.

Exercise 5:

Here, two fingers are required at the same time. Again, aim for a crisp, clear sound.

Exercise 6:

The 3rd finger on the 1st string, playing G and B (open 2nd string) together.

Picking strings together

After striking the strings the thumb rises up and back to begin again in a circular motion.
Keep the right hand relaxed and close to the strings.

In later lessons you will learn to pick using the right-hand finger tips.

Pieces for Lesson 3

22–23

Ave Maria

Bach/Gounod

Try either part of this piece, or play it as a duet with another guitarist.

Aim for a steady pulse and a smooth sound.

24–25

Gymnopédie No. 1

Satie

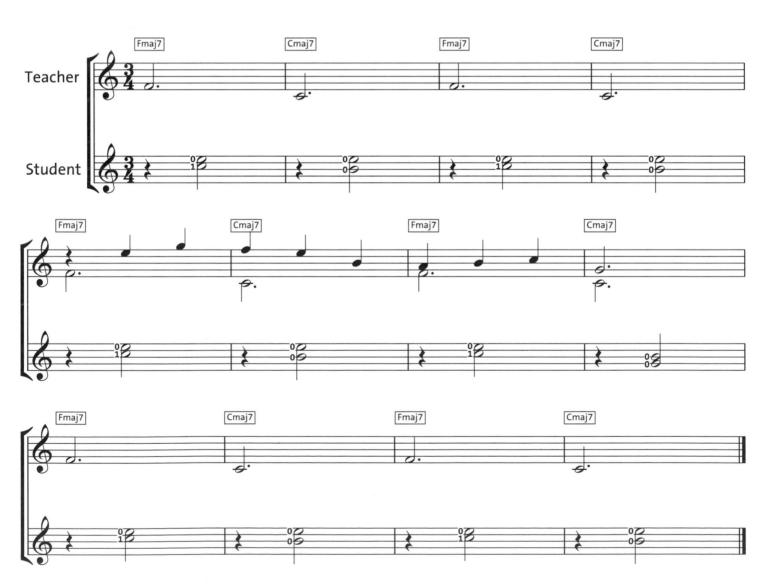

Pieces for Lesson 3

Frère Jacques

French Folk Song

Frè - re   Jac - ques   Frè - re   Jac - ques   Dor - mez - vous?   Dor - mez - vous?

Son-nez les ma - ti - nes,   Son-nez les ma - ti - nes.   Din, dan, don.   Din, dan, don.

I Know Where I'm Going

Scottish Ballad

1. **E and F on the 4th string**
2. **3-string chords: C, G7, and Dm**
3. **Repeat signs**
4. **Strum notation**
5. **Chord box diagrams**
6. **$\frac{2}{4}$ time signature**

New notes

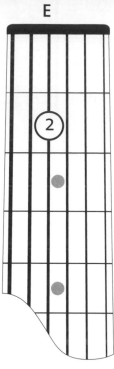

E

Finger 2 on 2nd fret, 4th string

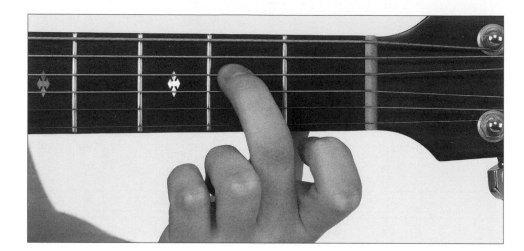

F

Finger 3 on 3rd fret, 4th string

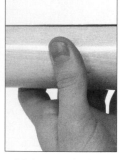

Make sure the fingers are supported by the thumb in the correct position on the back of the neck.

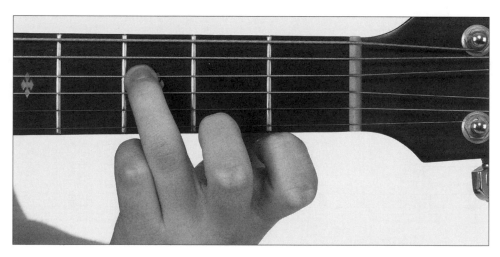

Exercises 1 & 2:

Try these two exercises using the 4th string.

Don't forget to support the hand shape with the thumb at the back of the guitar neck.

E D E D E D E

F D F D F D F

Chord box diagrams

The left-hand finger positions in a chord can be shown with dots on a picture of the fretboard.

Notice how the *chord box diagram* relates to the guitar neck, with the strings running straight down and the frets across the box. The **X** and **O** symbols above certain strings indicate either that a string is played open (**O**) or else not played (**X**).

Dm

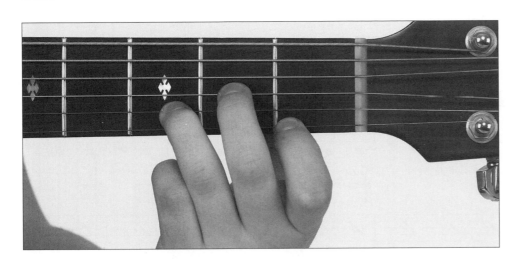
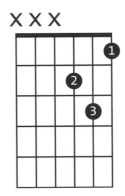

What does the "m" in Dm mean? Turn to lesson 9 for an explanation.

Strumming notation

Each beat for which a chord is strummed is written as a diagonal slash. In the three exercises that follow, each slash is worth a quarter note.

Exercise 3:

Remember to keep a steady beat, and use the thumb to strum gently down across the strings.

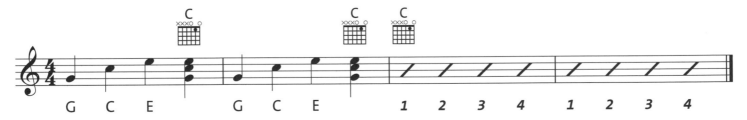

Exercise 4:

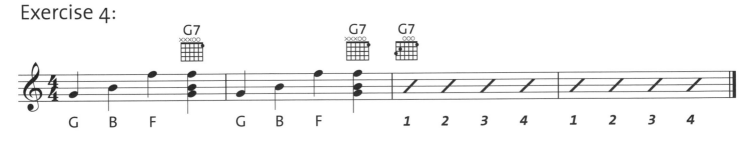

Exercise 5:

For the Dm chord, add an A on the 3rd string to the 2-note chord in Ex. 5, lesson 3.

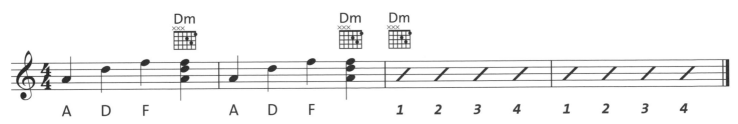

Pieces for Lesson 4

Can Can

Offenbach

This piece uses a new time signature: $\frac{2}{4}$. Each bar is worth two quarter notes.

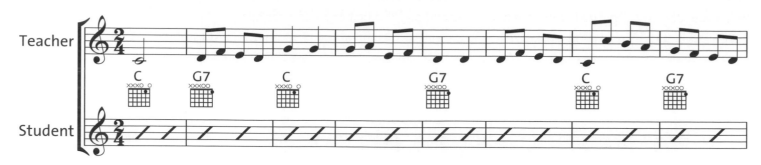

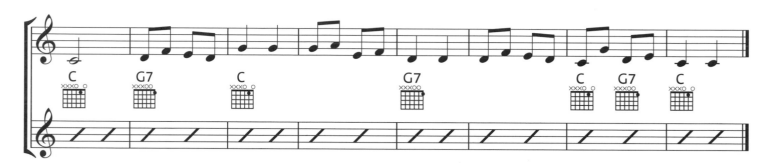

This sign 𝅗 is called a **pause** (or *fermata*). When this sign appears, the note should be held for longer than usual. The pause sign is sometimes found at the end of a piece of music.

Some Folks Do

Foster

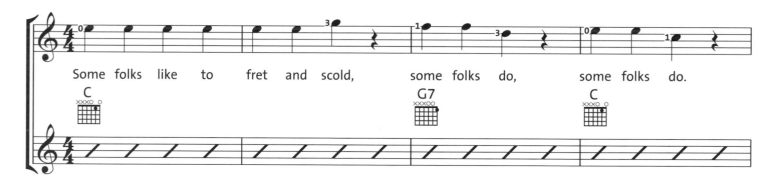

Some folks like to fret and scold, some folks do, some folks do.

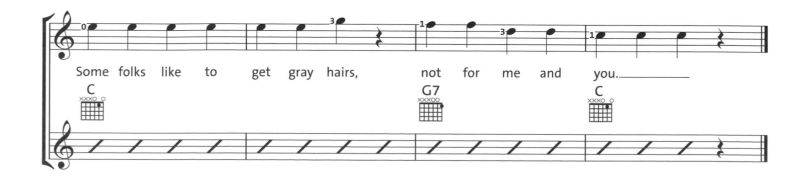

Some folks like to get gray hairs, not for me and you.

20

Pieces for Lesson 4

Santa Lucia

Cottrau

Look at the double dots at the end of bar 8: this is a **repeat sign**.

When you reach this sign, go back to the beginning and play the first eight bars again.

Notice also how bars 9 to 16 are enclosed in repeat signs: at the end of bar 16, return to the start of bar 9

and play again—but on the repeat, go straight into the *second ending*, skipping the *first ending*.

Repeat signs and different endings are a common way of saving space and paper!

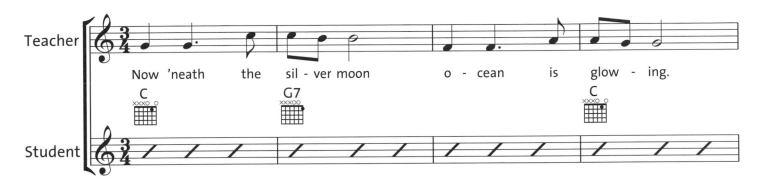

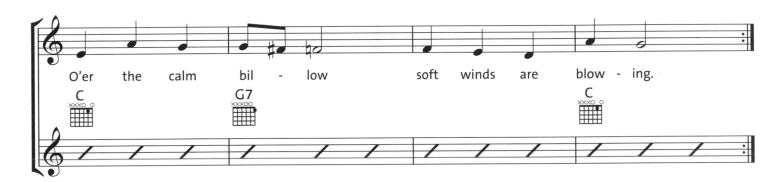

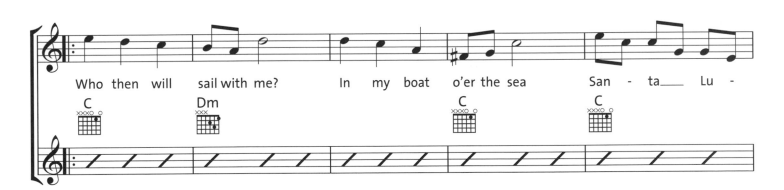

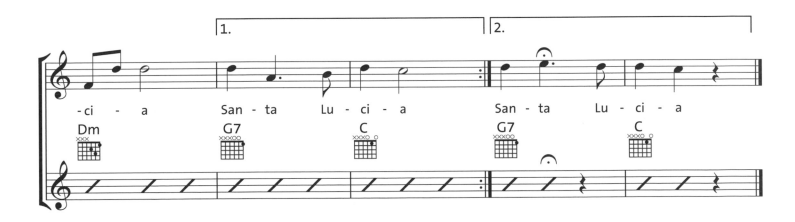

21

goals:

1. **The upbeat (anacrusis)**
2. **3-string chords: G, D7, and F**

3. **The tie**
4. **D.S. al Fine**

Upbeats

Music doesn't always start with a complete bar.

Some of the pieces in this lesson begin with a shorter bar (an **anacrusis**), which is balanced by another shorter bar at the end of the piece. These two bars together add up to one complete bar.

Where the anacrusis is worth a single beat, this is known as an **upbeat**.

New chords
D7

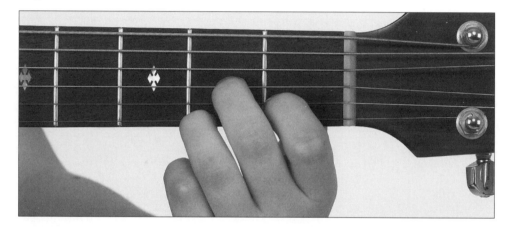
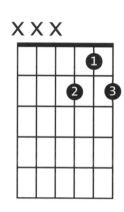

G

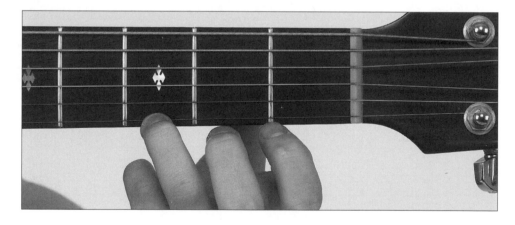
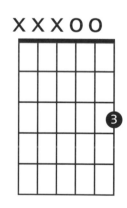

F

In this chord the 1st finger should form a bar across the top two strings on the first fret. This is shown by the arched symbol in the diagram. Roll the 1st finger onto the outside edge for the best contact—and don't squeeze too hard! Placement is more important than pressure here.

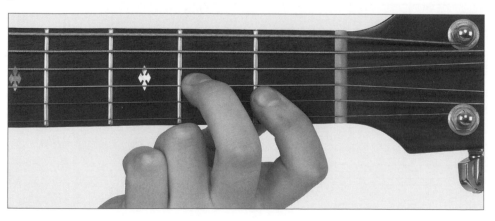
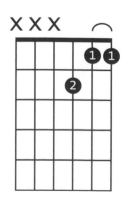

Exercise 1

The 3rd finger is used on the 1st string in both chords here. Try to keep the 3rd finger on the string throughout, sliding it into position rather than lifting and replacing each time.

Exercise 2:

Be sure to wait until both fingers are perfectly in position for the F chord before playing it.

Ties and tied notes

Two notes of the same pitch can be joined together to make a longer note by *tying* them together. A curved line is drawn from one to the other to show this. The note is then held on for the *combined value* of the two notes. This is usually needed if a note needs to carry into the next bar.

Here are some examples:

Is held for **3** beats   Is held for **6** beats

Exercise 3

Try working out the length of the notes in this exercise before playing, and keep a steady count as you go through it.

Keeping a steady beat is essential to playing and reading music.

Practice counting the bars and beats out loud when you play until you are confident that you are playing with a solid beat.

When reading a piece of music for the first time it is a good idea to check the key signature and to look for the highest and lowest notes. You can then make any awkward fingering changes as smoothly as possible.

Pieces for Lesson 5

She'll Be Comin' 'Round The Mountain American Traditional

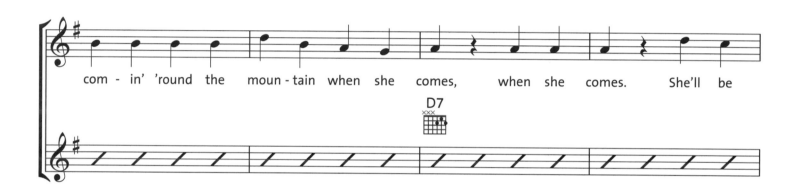

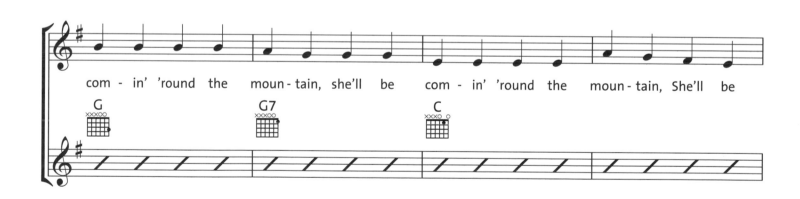

Pieces for Lesson 5

Grandfather's Clock

H. C. Work

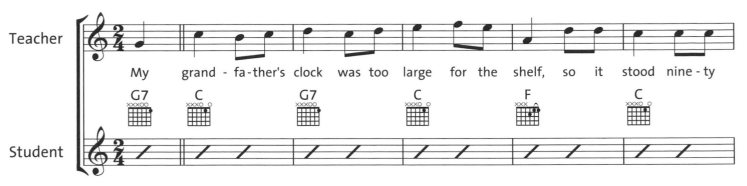

My grand-fa-ther's clock was too large for the shelf, so it stood nine-ty

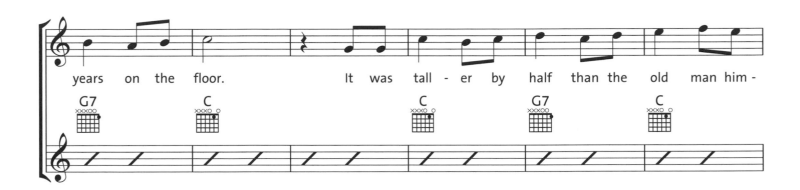

years on the floor. It was tall-er by half than the old man him-

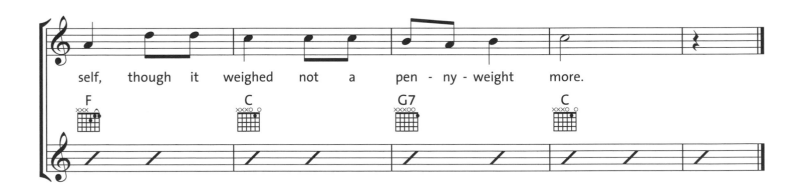

self, though it weighed not a pen-ny-weight more.

D.S. AL FINE

In "She'll Be Comin' 'Round The Mountain" a new device is used.

At the end of the piece *D.S. al Fine* is written. D.S. (short for *dal segno*, or *from the sign*) takes the music back to the ornate 𝄋 near the beginning of the piece.

Play from there until the *Fine* (finish).

D.S. al Fine therefore means "from the sign to the end."

Pieces for Lesson 5

Amazing Grace

Traditional

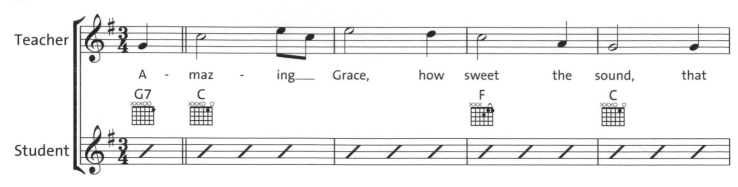

Teacher / Student

A - maz - ing__ Grace, how sweet the sound, that

G7   C   F   C

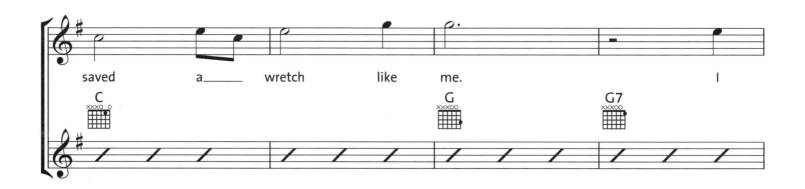

saved   a__ wretch like me.   I

C   G   G7

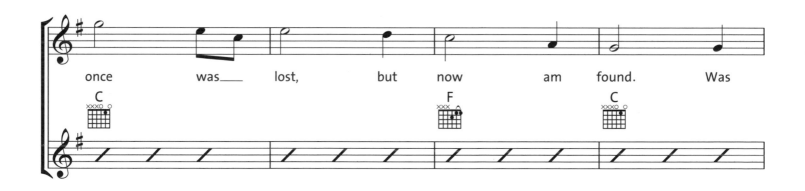

once   was__ lost, but now am found. Was

C   F   C

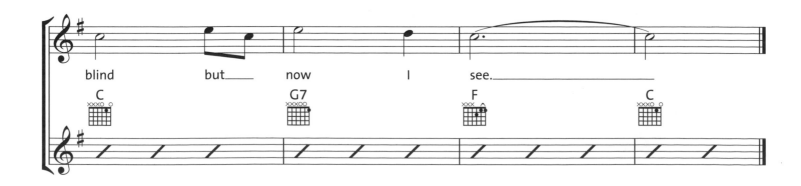

blind   but__ now I see.__

C   G7   F   C

1. Name the notes

Write the names of the following notes below each one.

(12)

2. Rhythmic values

Give the count of each note or rest.

(14)

3. Name the chords

Write the names of these chord symbols.

(10)

4. Guitar Parts

What are the names of the following parts of the guitar?

- The hole at the front of the body . . . .

- The long arm on which the fingerboard is mounted . . . .

- The knobs that change the tension of the strings . . . .

- The wires that divide the fingerboard into sections . . . .

(8)

5. D.S. al Fine

Describe what happens when D.S. al Fine is written.

(6)

Total (50)

1. **New notes F♯, C, and A**
2. **Tones and semitones**
3. **Key signatures**
4. **Major scale**
5. **Eighth notes**

New notes

F♯	F♯ high	C	A

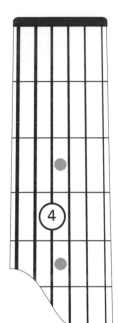   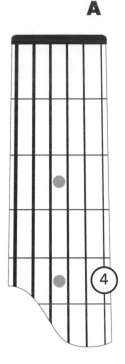

Finger 4 on 4th fret, 4th string

Finger 2 on 2nd fret, 1st string

Finger 3 on 3rd fret, 5th string

Finger 4 on 5th fret, 1st string

Tones and semitones

The frets divide the strings into intervals known as **semitones**.

Look at the way the notes you have learned so far are arranged: you will notice that some pairs, such as G and A, or D and E, have two semitones (one *tone*) between them, whereas other pairs, such as B and C, or E and F, are just one semitone apart.

The major scale

The notes of the major scale follow a particular pattern of intervals.

Most of the notes are a tone apart, but between the 3rd and 4th notes of the scale, and again between the 7th and 8th notes of the scale, the interval is only half as much: a semitone.

	Tone		Tone		Semitone		Tone		Tone		Tone		Semitone	
1		2			3	4			5		6		7	8

Sharps

Look at the F♯s on the previous page: they are both F raised a semitone.

The symbol ♯ (sharp) is used to raise the note by a semitone.

Try to find other examples on the fretboard, such as G♯, D♯, and C♯.

Exercise 1: C major scale

These are the notes played when starting on C and following the major scale sequence.

Exercise 2: G major scale

Here is the same scale, but this time starting on G.

Notice how, to preserve the sequence, the F is raised by a semitone to F♯.

New Notes

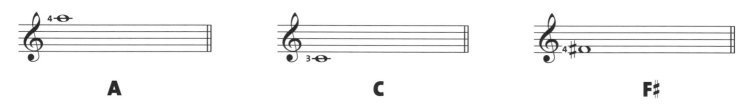

A   **C**   **F♯**

Key signatures

So far all the pieces you've played are in the key of C: they don't use any sharps.

The following pieces are in the key of G, which requires an F♯.

This is shown by the ♯ symbol at the beginning of the piece—known as the **key signature**.

Eighth notes

Eighth notes and an eighth-note rest

Eighth notes in pairs
(worth one quarter note per pair)

Eighth notes as a group
(a half note's worth)

Pieces for Lesson 6

42–43 *Streets Of Laredo*

American Traditional

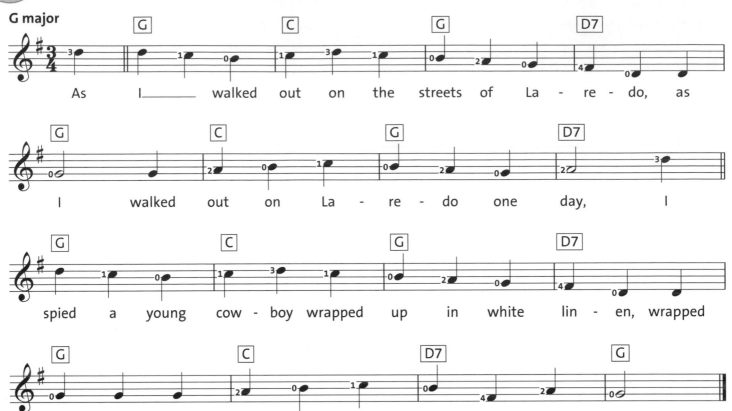

As I walked out on the streets of La - re - do, as
I walked out on La - re - do one day, I
spied a young cow - boy wrapped up in white lin - en, wrapped
up in white lin - en and cold as the clay.

44–45 *Botany Bay*

Australian Traditional

Sing-ing too - ral - li oo - ral - li ad - di - ty,_____ sing-ing

too - ral - li oo - ra - li - ay._____ Sing - ing

too - ral - li, oo - ra - li ad - di - ty,_____ for we're

bound for the Bo - ta - ny Bay._____

goals:

1. **4-note chords G, D7, C, F, and G7**
2. **D.C. al Fine**
3. **Dotted quarter notes**

New 4-note chords

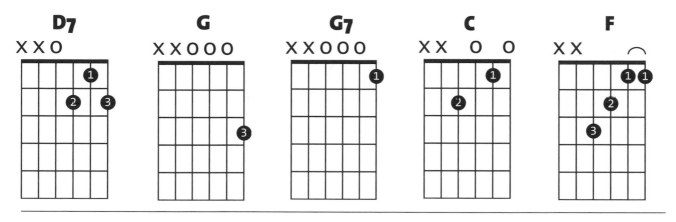

C: To add another string to the C chord, the 2nd fret on the 4th string is played with the 2nd finger.

F: Add the 3rd finger on the 3rd fret of the 4th string for this 4-note version of F.

The 4-note versions of these chords are extended versions of the 3-note shapes you have already learned. Eventually you will learn 5-note and even 6-note versions of some of these chords.

Exercise 1: Country Gardens

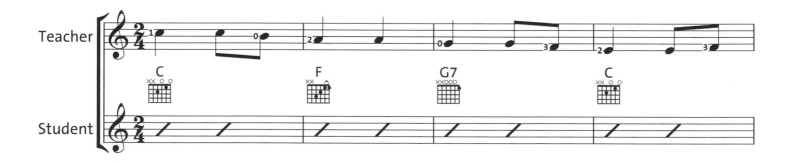

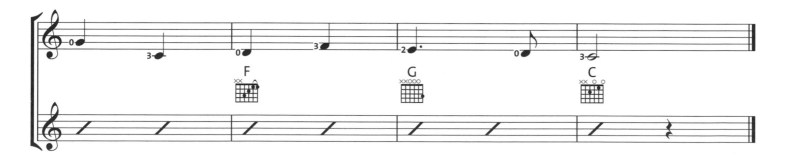

Dotted quarter notes

As discussed in lesson 3, a dot after a note increases its value by half.

This is true of any note value, and in the following piece a dotted quarter note is coupled with an eighth note to make two complete beats.

31

Home On The Range

American Traditional

Pieces for Lesson 7

Early One Morning

English Folk Song

 48–49

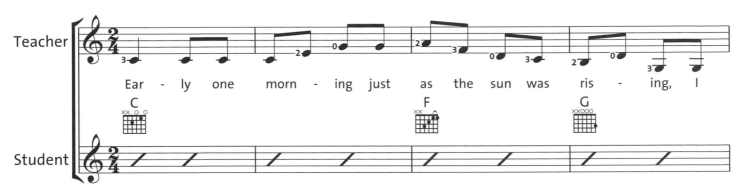

Ear - ly one morn - ing just as the sun was ris - ing, I

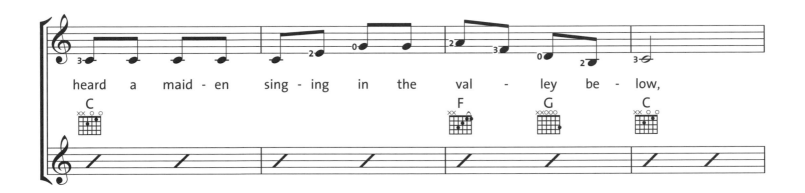

heard a maid - en sing - ing in the val - ley be - low,

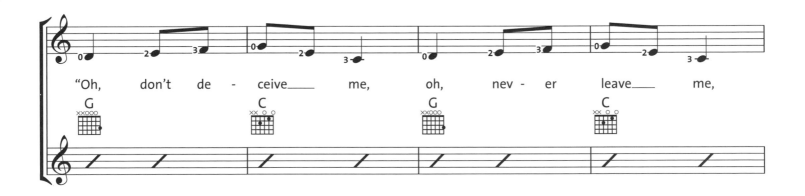

"Oh, don't de - ceive___ me, oh, nev - er leave___ me,

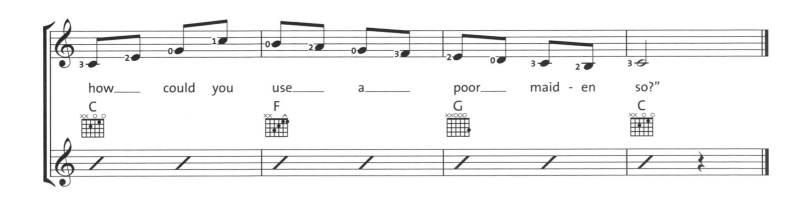

how___ could you use___ a___ poor___ maid - en so?"

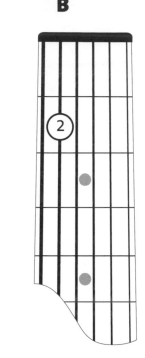

Lesson 8

goals:

1. **B on the A string**
2. **F and G on the bottom E string**
3. **Bar repeat sign**

New notes

B   **F**   **G**

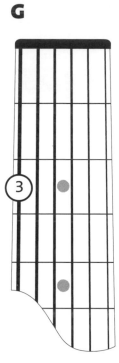

Finger 2 on 2nd fret, 5th string

Finger 1 on 1st fret, 6th string

Finger 3 on 3rd fret, 6th string

The low notes introduced in this lesson are great for basslines, an important part of guitar technique. Play the following exercise with the thumb and keep a steady beat.

The ⁒ symbol shows that the bar is a repeat of the previous bar. It is often used in guitar music where a pattern repeats across several bars.

Exercise 1:

In these next two exercises, aim for a smooth movement in the left hand. You might find it tricky to reach the 6th string at first: make sure your left-hand thumb is in the correct position and that the guitar is sitting upright.

Exercises 2 & 3:

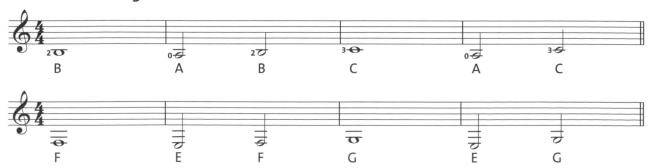

Pieces for Lesson 8

Song Of The Volga Boatmen

Russian Traditional

Dixie

Emmett

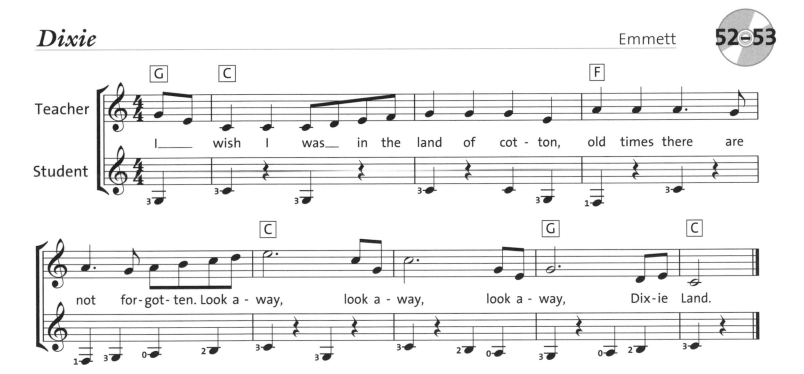

The Dalston Drag

goals:

1. **Dynamics**
2. **5-string chords C and Am**
3. **6-string chords G7, G, and Em**

New chords

C	Am	G7	G	Em
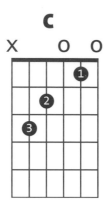	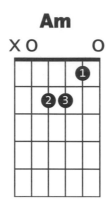	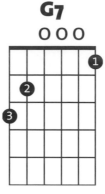	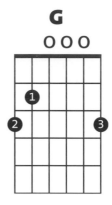	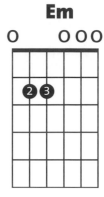

C: The basis of this chord is the same as the 4-note C chord in lesson 7, with the addition of the 3rd finger on the 3rd fret of the 5th string.

Am: The 1st and 2nd fingers are in the same position as for the C chord. Now just add the 3rd finger on the 2nd fret of the 3rd string.

G7: Stretch out to place the 3rd finger on the bottom string and the 2nd finger on the 5th string before placing the 1st finger on the top string.

G: Place the 1st finger on the 5th string, and the 2nd finger on the 6th, then put the 3rd finger on the top string.

Em: The second finger is placed on the 5th string, with the 3rd finger on the 4th string.

MINOR CHORDS

The "m" in Am and Em stands for *minor*.
Play these chords and compare them with C and G. You will find that the minor chords sound somehow darker and more melancholy than the others.
C and G are *major* chords, and sound brighter.
Where a chord name has no "m" after the letter, it is a major chord. D and F, for example, are also major chords, whereas the Dm learned in lesson 4 is minor.

Dynamics

Music uses Italian words to describe how loudly or quietly to play.

These words or abbreviations are called "dynamic markings."

Piano (written as *p*) = **quiet**   *Mezzo forte* (written as *mf*) = **moderately loud**   *Forte* (written as *f*) = **loud**

Pieces for Lesson 9

Away In A Manger

Kirkpatrick

A - way in a___ man - ger, no___ crib for His bed. The___

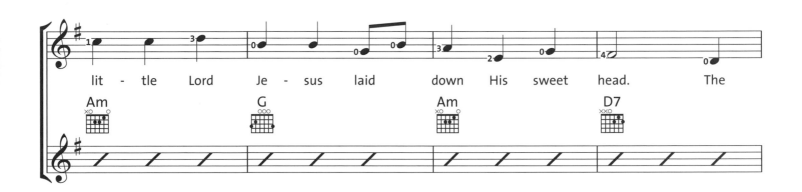

lit - tle Lord Je - sus laid down His sweet head. The

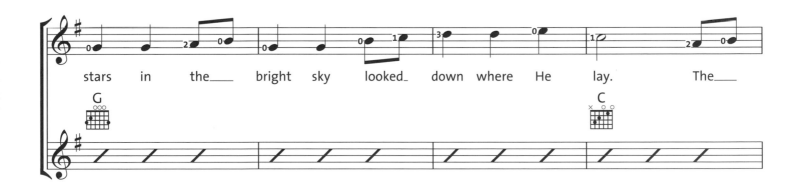

stars in the___ bright sky looked_ down where He lay. The___

lit - tle Lord Je - sus a - sleep on the hay.

Pieces for Lesson 9

58-59 *Jingle Bells*

Traditional

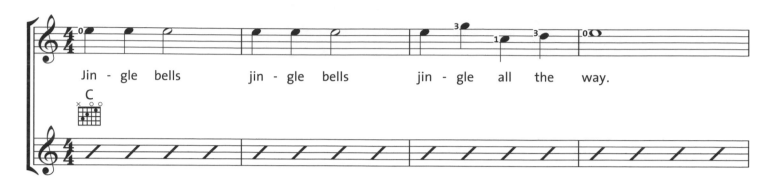

Jin - gle bells   jin - gle bells   jin - gle all the way.

C

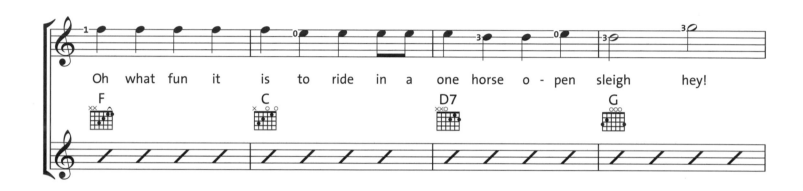

Oh what fun it is to ride in a one horse o - pen sleigh hey!

F   C   D7   G

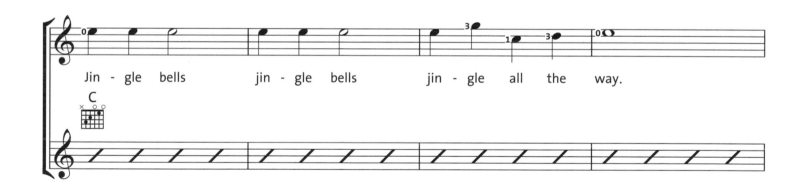

Jin - gle bells   jin - gle bells   jin - gle all the way.

C

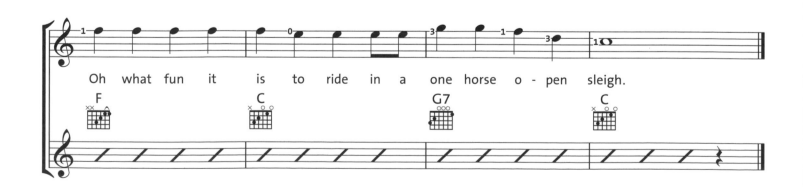

Oh what fun it is to ride in a one horse o - pen sleigh.

F   C   G7   C

Pieces for Lesson 9

O Come, All Ye Faithful

Wade

Notice the dynamic markings in this piece.

Towards the end the piece is quiet, growing through moderately loud, to loud at the finish.

1. **Strumming in eighth notes**
2. **Strumming notation**

Strumming

Up to now, you have strummed down across the strings once on every beat.

Strumming up in-between creates more possibilities for rhythmic variety.

Downstrum

Upstrum

Strumming should be light and relaxed, using the backs of the fingers and thumb. Try to rotate the wrist—not the elbow—to move the hand across the strings. Imagine you are holding a softball to keep the thumb and fingers in a nice rounded position.

Try to keep the hand close to the strings, steering the fingers and thumb very carefully as you turn the wrist.

The downstrum is played with the back of the fingertips: the finger nails lightly stroke the strings.

The upstrum is played with the back of the thumb nail.

Experiment by varying the speed or pressure of the strokes until the strings sing out together crisply.

In the following exercises arrows are used to show downstrums ↓ and upstrums ↑

To warm up, try exercise 1, strumming down once on each beat with an Em chord using the backs of the fingers in a light brushing motion.

Exercise 1:

Now play the same thing, but this time brush up with the back of the thumb in-between the downstrokes.

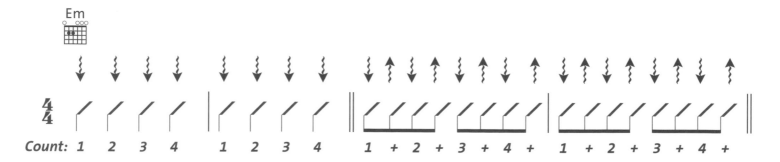

Count: 1   2   3   4   1   2   3   4   1 + 2 + 3 + 4 +   1 + 2 + 3 + 4 +

40

Finally, try this version: here you should move the hand up and down across the strings, but only make contact when the notation requires a strum.

Keep going up-down-up-down all the way through, even where no strum is needed.

Exercise 2:

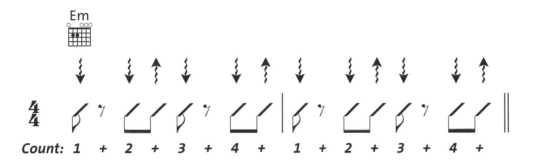

Count: 1 + 2 + 3 + 4 + 1 + 2 + 3 + 4 +

Pieces for Lesson 10

The Drunken Sailor

Sea Shanty

Now it's time to put all this strumming into practice.

Notice how, in each of the three following pieces, the strumming rhythm remains the same from bar to bar.

Try to make the strums sound constant and steady, while remembering to begin every new chord right at the beginning of the bar.

It might help to memorize each piece in sections so you can concentrate on playing rather than reading.

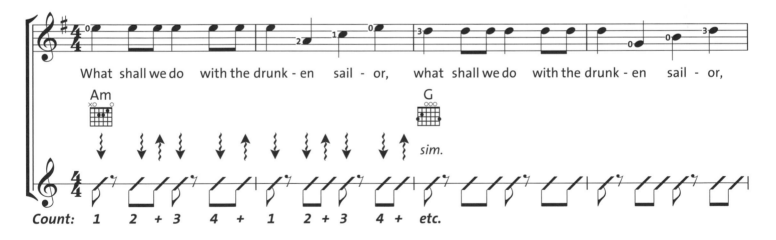

What shall we do with the drunk - en sail - or, what shall we do with the drunk - en sail - or,

Count: 1 2 + 3 4 + 1 2 + 3 4 + etc.

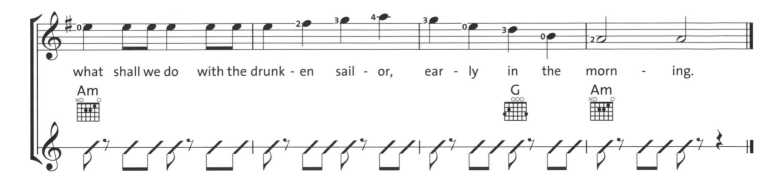

what shall we do with the drunk - en sail - or, ear - ly in the morn - ing.

Pieces for Lesson 10

Yellow Rose Of Texas

J.K.

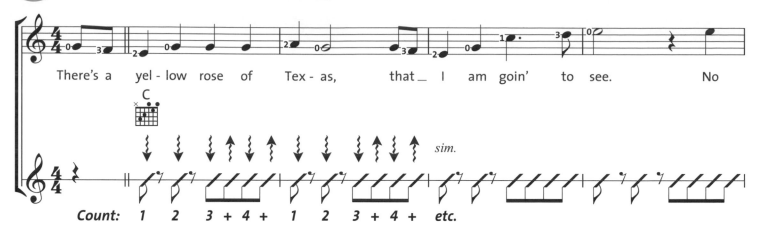

There's a yel-low rose of Tex-as, that I am goin' to see. No

Count: 1 2 3 + 4 + 1 2 3 + 4 + etc.

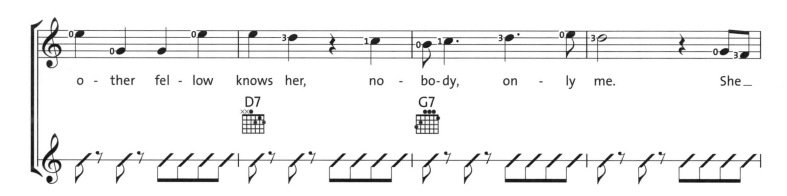

o - ther fel-low knows her, no - bo-dy, on - ly me. She

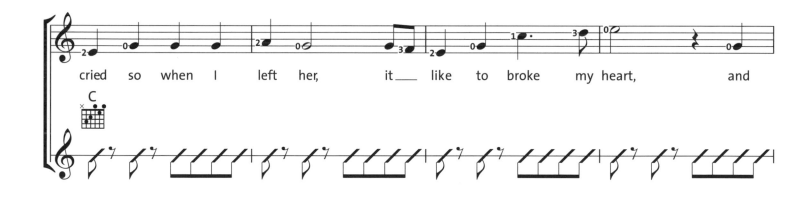

cried so when I left her, it like to broke my heart, and

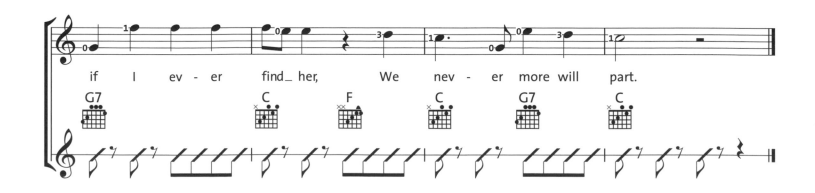

if I ev - er find her, We nev - er more will part.

test:

for Lessons 6 to 10

1. Name the notes

Write the names of the following notes below each one.

(12)

2. Play the rhythm

Clap or tap this rhythm.

(5)

3. Name the chords

Write the names of these chord symbols.

(10)

4. Fill in the blanks

Draw in the diagrams for the following chords.

D⁷   G   C

(6)

5. Symbols

What do these signs mean?   *mp*   ./.   :‖

            Sim   ♯   *f*

(12)

6. Scale intervals

Write in the correct sequence of intervals for a major scale.

(5)

Total **(50)**

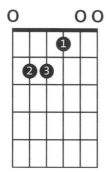

goals:

1. **Full chords E, A, and D**
2. **Reading tablature**
3. **Fingerpicking**
4. **Chord families**

New chords

E

On the E chord, the first finger is added to the Em shape already studied.

A

It's important to place the fingers accurately here to allow all the fingertips to find their correct position.

D

This is a completely different fingering than D7.

Chord families

Often a song will use a group of chords that "relate": many songs use exactly the same set of chords.

The most common chords in a particular key are the chords which have their bass notes on the first, fourth, and fifth notes of the scale.

Here are all the simple three-note chords in the key of C. The I, IV, and V chords are all major, and are the most common chords to use within a key.

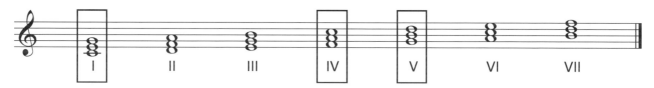

In the key of C, these are C, F, and G. In the key of G they would be G, C, and D.

Roman numerals are used to describe the position of each chord within a key, so these chords would be called I, IV, and V. Often chord V is a "7" chord: so in C, for instance, G would become G7 ; in G, chord V would be D7 rather than plain D.

Fingerpicking

The right-hand thumb plays the bass strings while the 1st, 2nd, and 3rd fingers play the upper strings. The 4th finger is not used in picking. Try to make smooth, relaxed strokes with the fingers and thumb.

If your right-hand nails are tough and long enough (they just need to peek over the fingertips), use them for a brighter, louder sound. Otherwise, use the tips of the fingers.

Look at the exercise below: you will see it is written in a different type of notation called **tablature**, often used to show fingerpicking. Each line represents a string on the guitar, and the numbers show which frets the left-hand fingers should be on. The letters refer to right-hand fingers.

In classical guitar music, fingers are indicated by their Spanish names.

t = thumb—sometimes written as *p* (pulgar)   *m* (medio) = 2nd finger

i (indio) = 1st finger   *a* = (anulo) 3rd finger

Exercise 1:

Play either the 4th, 5th, or 6th string with the thumb at the beginning of each bar (depending on the chord), and follow with each of the three fingers in turn on the 3rd, 2nd, and 1st strings.

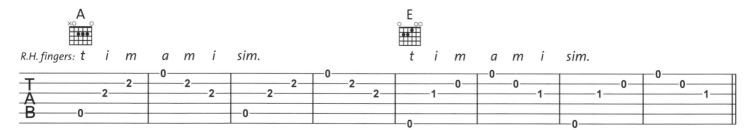

Exercise 2:

This time, with three beats in the bar, a pattern is made in two-bar sections.

You could think of this as *timami* and remember it that way.

Sim, or *simile*, indicates that you should continue in a similar fashion.

Exercise 3:

Aim for a smooth sound, and think of the pattern as a single shape rather than as lots of little picks.

The arrow across the notes in the final bar indicates a strum.

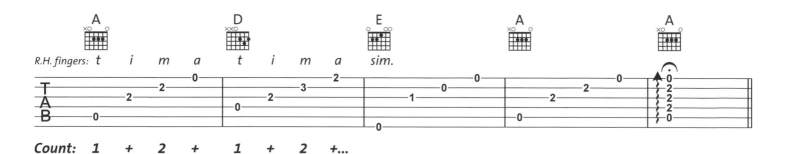

Pieces for Lesson 11

For the final third of this book, left-hand fingerings for melodies have been removed.

As you get to each new piece, spend a moment working out the most logical fingerings for yourself based on the scales and exercises studied so far.

Scarborough Fair

English Traditional

Play the top (melody) part in standard notation or the bottom (picking) part in tablature.

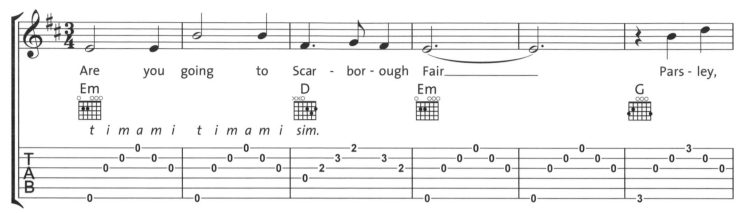

Count: *1 + 2 + 3 +   1 + 2 + 3 +*

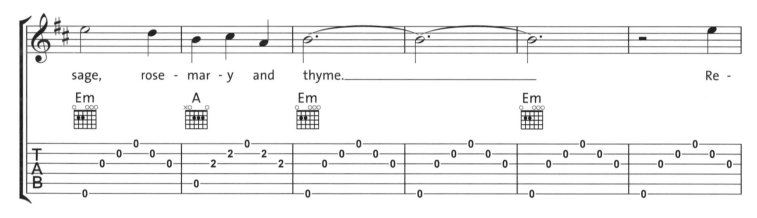

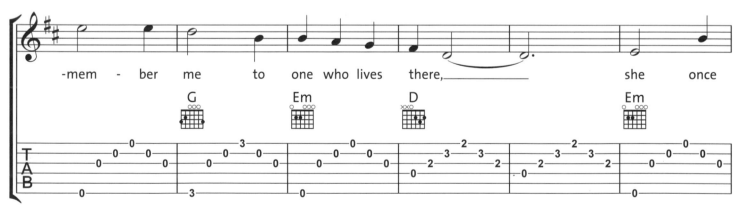

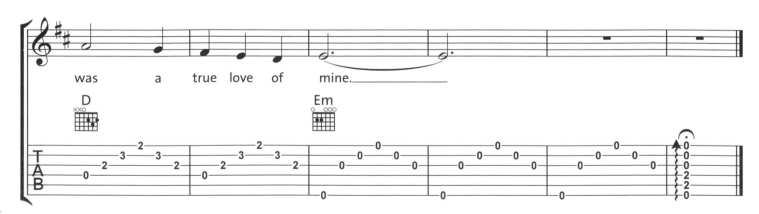

46

Pieces for Lesson 11

Amazing Grace

Traditional

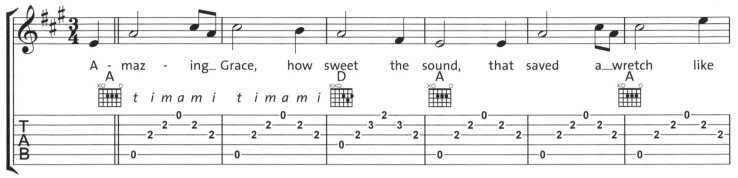

Count: 1 + 2 + 3 +   1 + 2 + 3 +

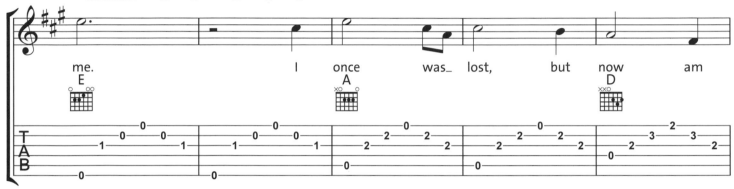

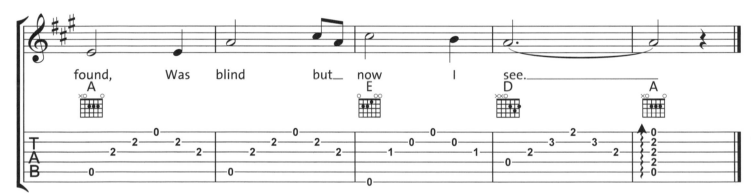

Oh! Susannah

Foster

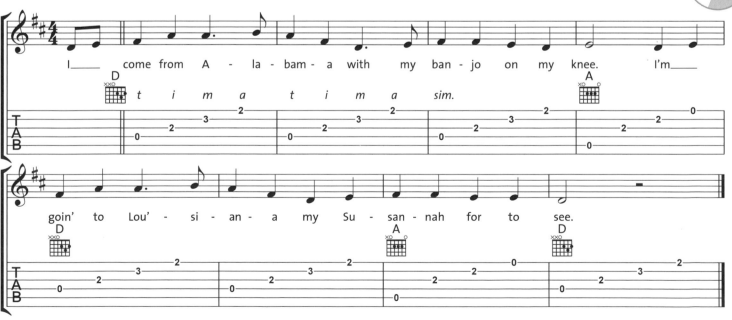

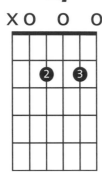

1. **A7 and E7**
2. **Bass pick strumming**
3. **Alternating bass**
4. **D major scale**

New chords

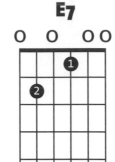

A7

X O O O

E7

O O O O

Use the same fingering as you would for E, but leave the 3rd finger out. Be sure to let the D string ring out clearly.

Bass pick strumming

Many guitar picking and strumming techniques aim to emulate, or reflect, the sound of a band. Bass picking gives a typical "boom-ching boom-ching" feel that would normally be played by the drums, bass and piano together. Try to keep this sound in mind as you work through this lesson.

Rather than strumming four beats to the bar, you can play with more rhythmic variety by adding single notes into the pattern.

The most important single note in the chord is the **root** (the note after which the chord is named, and usually the bottom note) and this note can be played together with strums to provide interest.

Exercise 1:

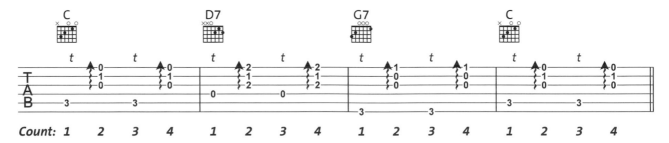

Alternating bass

When picking bass notes on the 1st and 3rd beats of the bar, further variety can be achieved by alternating the *root* with another note of the chord. In exercise 2, notice how the bass notes shift from one string to another in each bar.

Exercise 2:

If possible, you should alternate between the root and the next string down on the same fret (if the root string is open, the lower one will be open too). Where the root is already on the bottom string, you'll need to go up for the alternate note. For an E chord, go up to the 5th string; and for a G chord, go up to the 4th string.

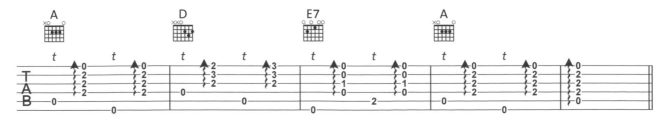

D major scale

As with C major and G major, the D major scale follows the **T T S T T T S** sequence outlined below.

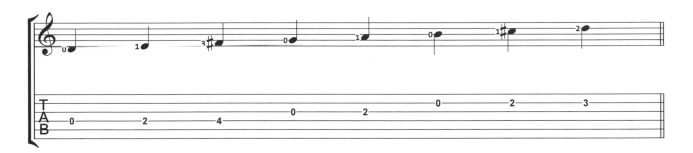

| Tone | Tone | Semitone | Tone | Tone | Tone | Semitone |
| 1 | 2 | 3 | 4 | 5 | 6 | 7 | 8 |

Exercise 3:

The D major scale requires a key signature of two sharps: F♯ and C♯.

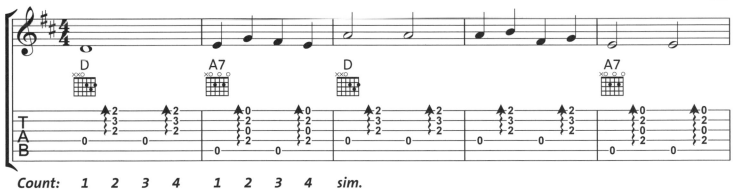

Pieces for Lesson 12

Can Can

Offenbach

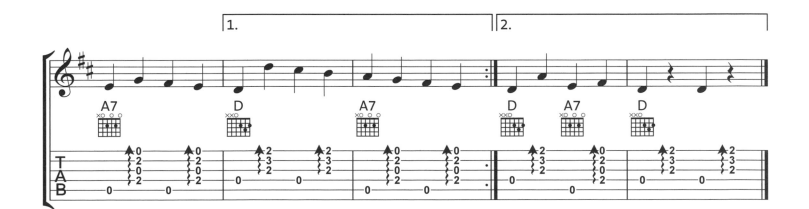

Count: 1   2   3   4   1   2   3   4   sim.

Pieces for Lesson 12

74-75

Streets Of Laredo

American Traditional

This piece is in triple time, that is, three beats to the bar. The *boom-ching* feel now becomes *boom-ching-ching*.

Aim to keep the bass note at the beginning of the bar nice and solid.
The strums that follow the bass note can be light, and you might even try inserting some upstrums in between for variety.

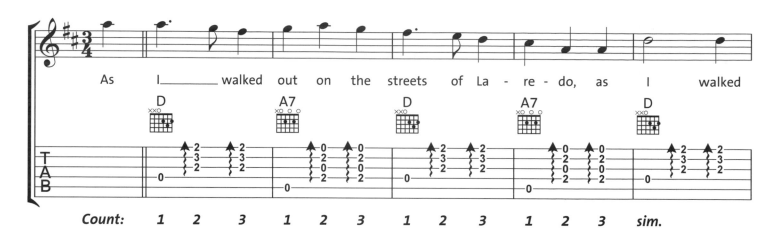

As I_____walked out on the streets of La - re - do, as I walked

Count: 1 2 3 1 2 3 1 2 3 1 2 3 **sim.**

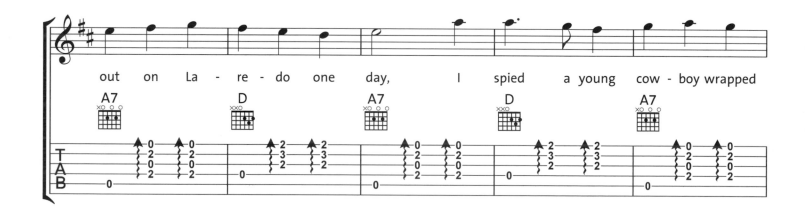

out on La - re - do one day, I spied a young cow - boy wrapped

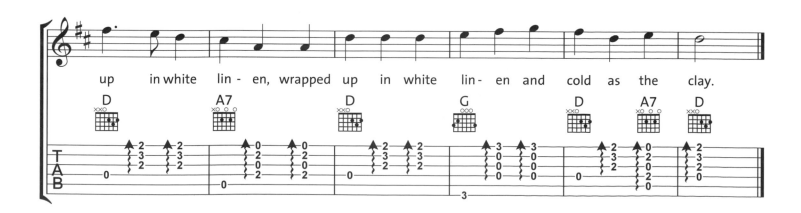

up in white lin - en, wrapped up in white lin - en and cold as the clay.

50

Pieces for Lesson 12

Banks Of The Ohio

American Traditional

This piece uses the same alternating bass picking as exercise 2. If you remember a couple of simple rules, this will soon become a natural part of your accompaniment technique.

If the root note is on the 4th or 5th string, simply alternate to the next string **down** on the same fret.

If the root note is on the 6th string, you'll need to alternate **up**: for E, alternate from the 6th to the 5th string; and for G, alternate from the 6th to the 4th string.

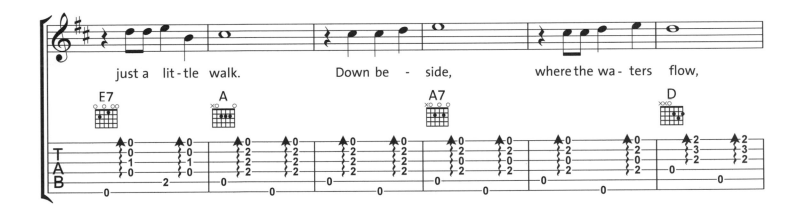

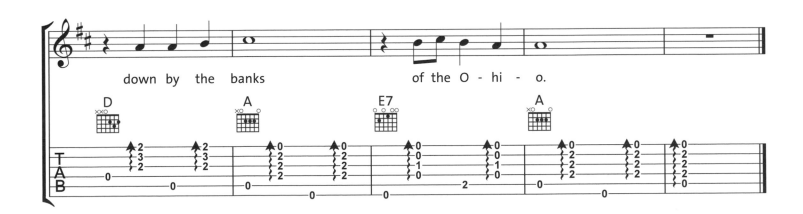

1. B♭ and C♯ on the 5th string
2. F♯ and G♯ on the 6th sting

3. B7
4. Bassline workout

New notes

B♭

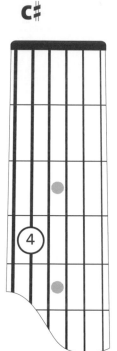

C♯

F♯

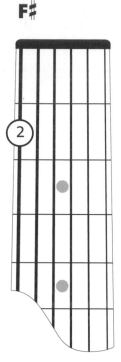

G♯

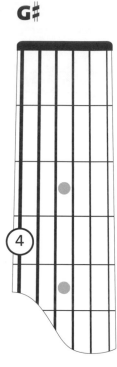

Finger 1 on 1st fret, 5th string

Finger 4 on 4th fret, 5th string

Finger 1 on 2nd fret, 6th string

Finger 4 on 4th fret, 6th string

New chord
B7

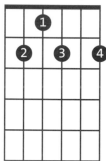

The 1st, 2nd and 3rd fingers are grouped just as they are for D7—but two strings lower.

Once they are in place, carefully position the 4th finger on the 2nd fret of the top (1st) string.

In the following pieces you will see the bass notes written out as a melody—use the TAB to help you see where the notes should be played.

This kind of bassline "walks" up and down, using mainly chord notes with some other notes from the scale to help step between the chord notes.

Exercise 1:

This is a typical bassline for boogie or rock'n'roll. Notice the D: this is the "7" of E7.

Exercise 2:

Here's the same thing for A7—with a G for the "7."

Exercise 3:

And finally the same walking bassline for D7. This time you'll begin on the 4th string; the line "walks" right up into the 2nd string.

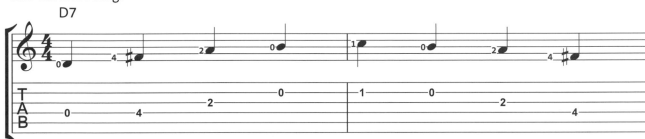

An octave is the distance between two notes with the same letter name but eight scale notes apart. The open bottom E string is an octave lower than the E on the 2nd fret of the 4th string, and two octaves lower than the open top E string.

Pieces for Lesson 13

12-Bar Boogie

Blackwell

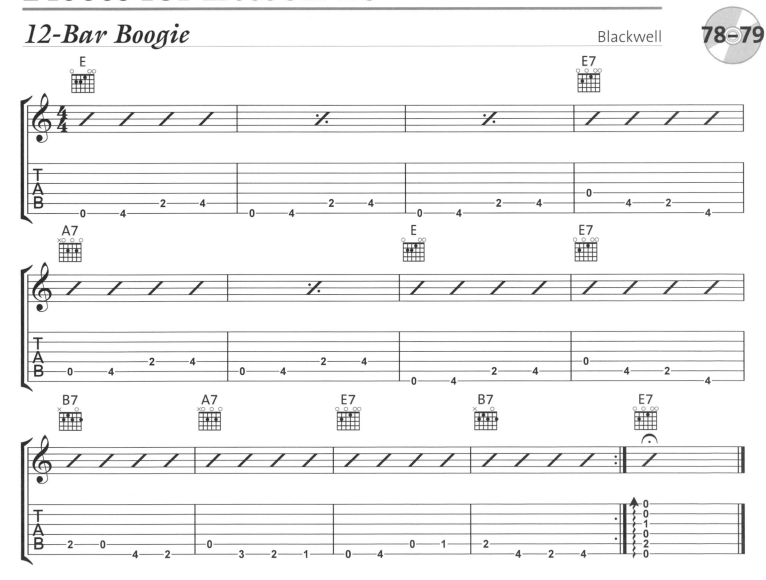

Pieces for Lesson 13

80–81

Mama Don't Allow

American Traditional

Aim for a firm and steady feel: the bassline needs to be right on the beat.

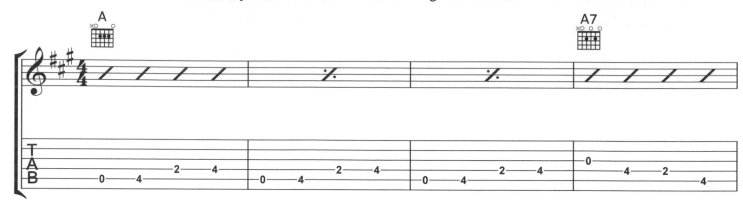

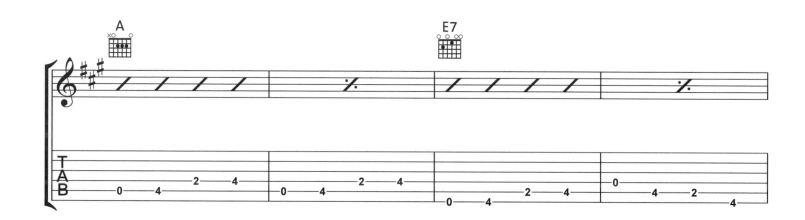

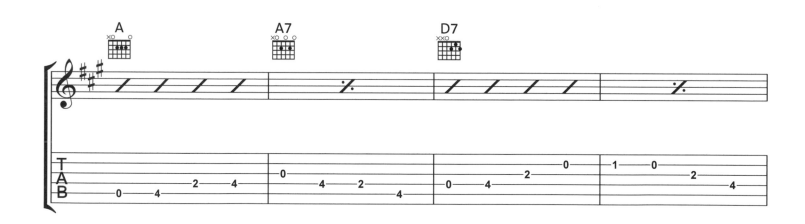

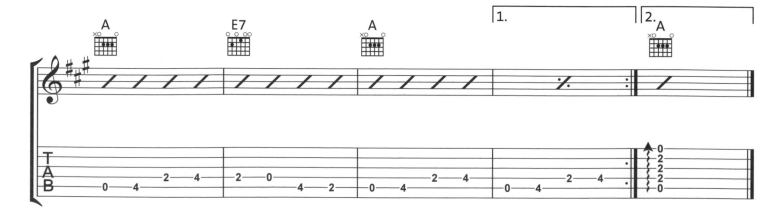

goals:

1. **More strumming patterns**
2. **Rhythm notation**

3. **C7**
4. **F major scale**

New chord: C7

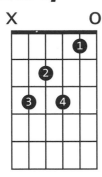

C7 is just like C, but with the 4th finger on the 3rd fret of the 3rd string.

More strumming

The strumming patterns in lesson 10 omitted certain upstrums to create interesting rhythms.

In the following exercises you will leave out some downstrums: this gives a feeling of pushing forward.

Exercise 1:

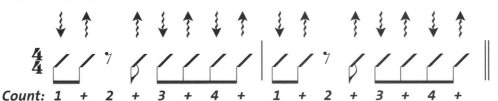

Count: 1 + 2 + 3 + 4 + 1 + 2 + 3 + 4 +

Practice these carefully with your favorite chords, and remember to count a steady pulse.

Exercise 2:

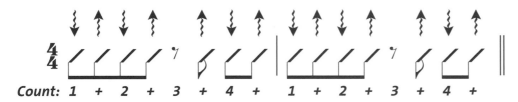

Count: 1 + 2 + 3 + 4 + 1 + 2 + 3 + 4 +

Exercise 3:

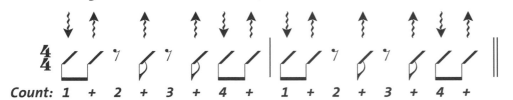

Count: 1 + 2 + 3 + 4 + 1 + 2 + 3 + 4 +

F major scale

Beginning a major scale on F requires the 4th note, B, to be flatted in order to preserve the **T T S T T T S** sequence.

String: ④ ③ ② ①

Pieces for Lesson 14

Jamaica Farewell

Caribbean Traditional

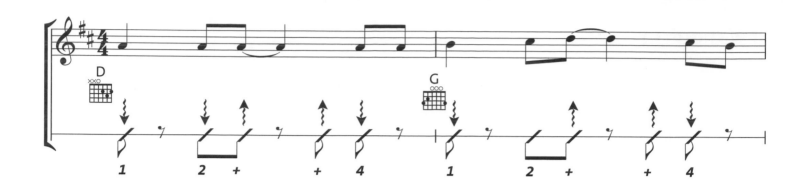

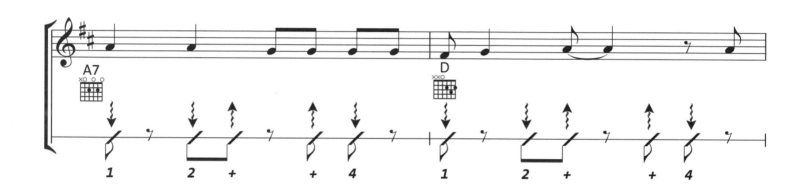

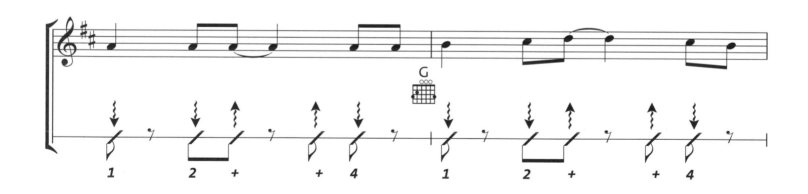

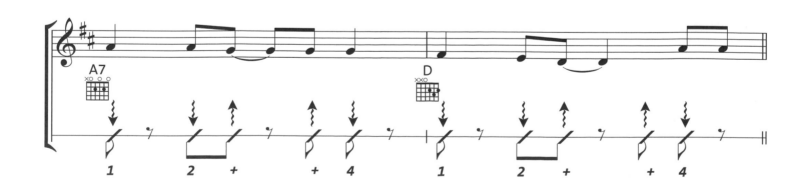

Remember: keep the strumming hand moving up and down on each beat even where no strum is required.

Remember: keep the strumming hand moving up and down on each beat even where no strum is required.

This way you'll keep a steady beat and always be strumming down on the *onbeat* and up on the *offbeat*.

Watch out for the change of strumming rhythm in the second part of this tune!

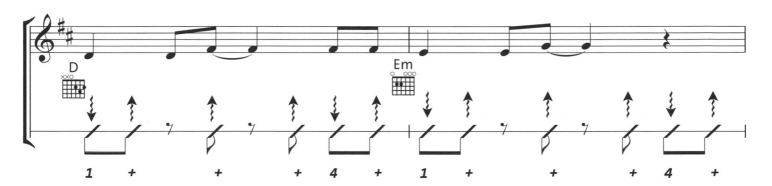

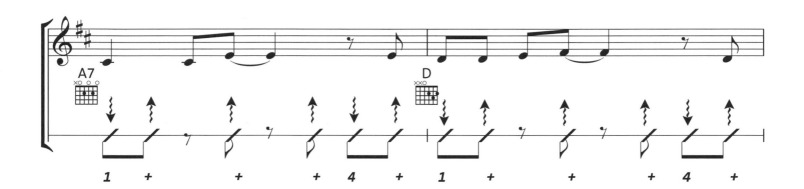

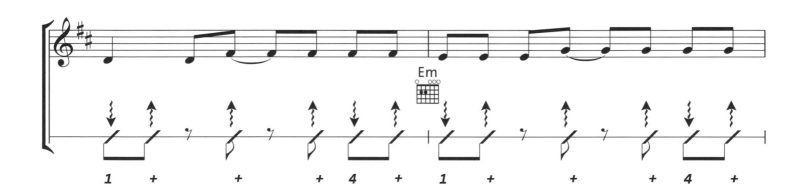

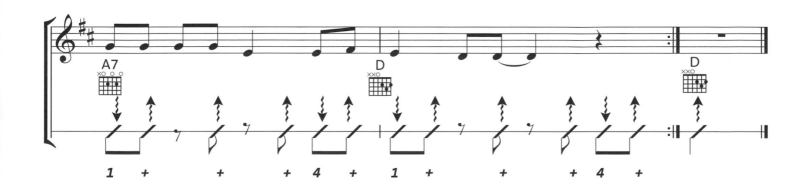

Pieces for Lesson 14

This Train Is Bound For Glory

Spiritual

84-85

In this piece, the strumming part is written in TAB, complete with an alternating bass.

Try to emphasize the 1st and 3rd beats to create a steady bassline. It might help to work out which strings are needed for the alternating bass before playing through the song.

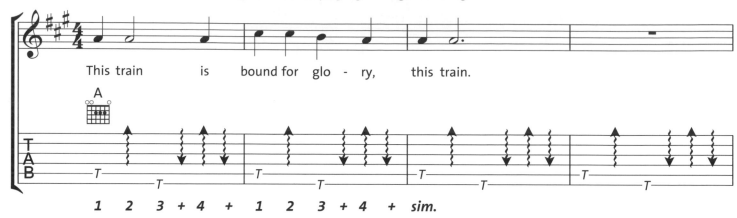

This train is bound for glo - ry, this train.

1 2 3 + 4 + 1 2 3 + 4 + sim.

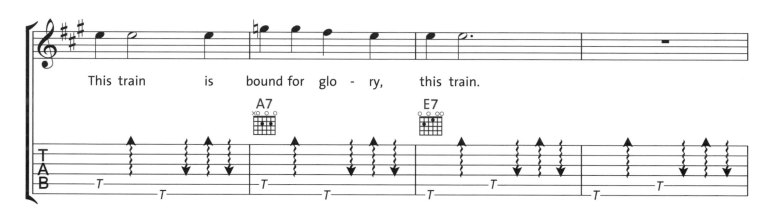

This train is bound for glo - ry, this train.

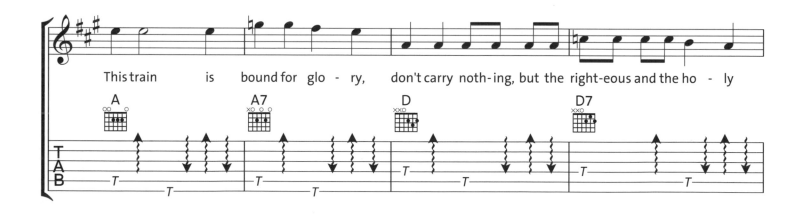

This train is bound for glo - ry, don't carry noth-ing, but the right-eous and the ho - ly

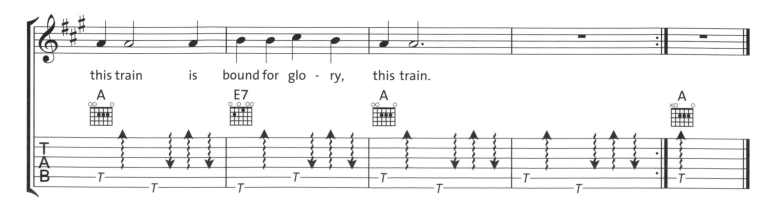

this train is bound for glo - ry, this train.

goals:

1. **Advanced picking**
2. **Passing bass notes**
3. **Ritardando**

Picking with two fingers together

In the following pieces, the fingers are often required to pluck more than one string at the same time.

Make sure the correct finger is chosen for each string to avoid confusion and keep the flow.

Generally, for fingerpicking, the three fingers play the top three strings as shown, while the thumb plays the bass strings.

Passing bass notes

Often, a bassline will include notes that help to "move" from one chord to the next.

Look at "Greensleeves," for example: in the first bar the bassline walks up from A.

The B is the note that steps between A and C. In bar 3 an F♯ is played to step between G and the E in the following bar.

These intermediate notes are known as *passing notes*. "Greensleeves" includes many passing notes and alternating bass notes that give an interesting countermelody to the tune.

Pieces for Lesson 15

Greensleeves

Attributed to Henry VIII

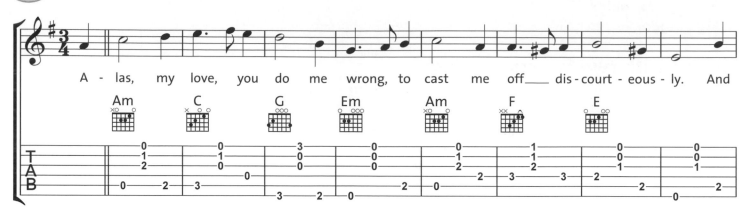

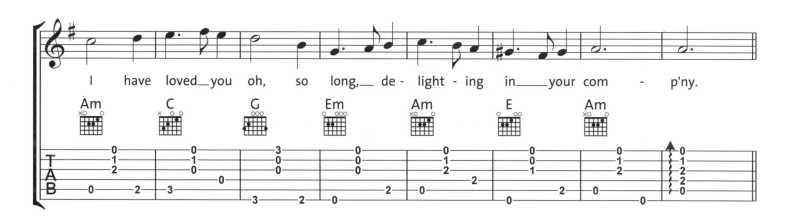

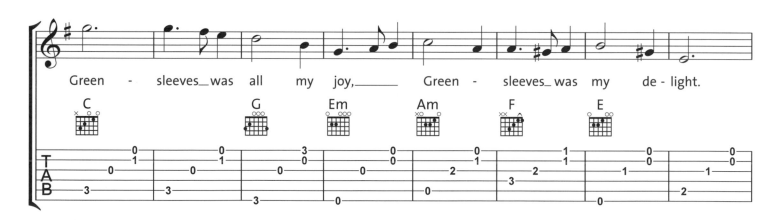

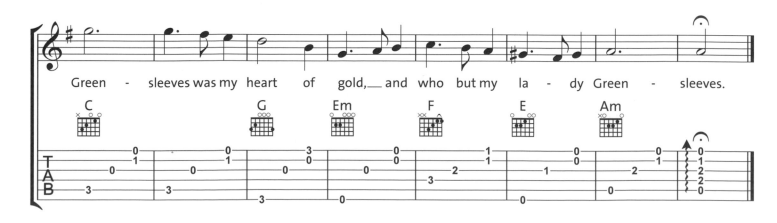

Pieces for Lesson 15

God Rest Ye Merry Gentlemen Traditional

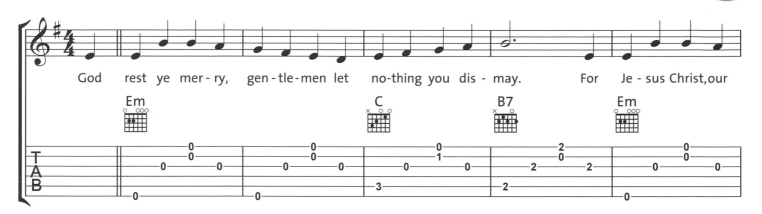

God rest ye mer-ry, gen-tle-men let no-thing you dis-may. For Je-sus Christ, our

Em   C   B7   Em

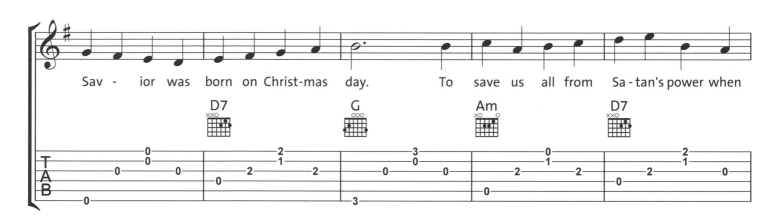

Sav - ior was born on Christ-mas day. To save us all from Sa-tan's power when

D7   G   Am   D7

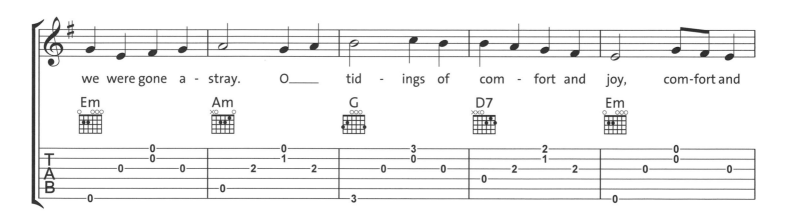

we were gone a-stray. O___ tid-ings of com-fort and joy, com-fort and

Em   Am   G   D7   Em

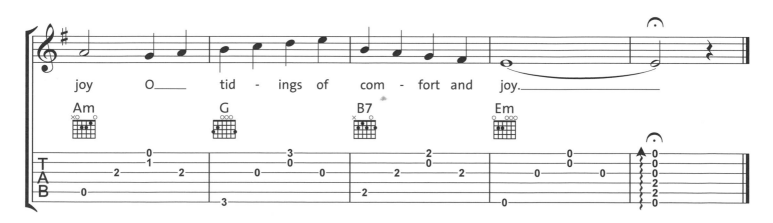

joy O___ tid-ings of com-fort and joy.___

Am   G   B7   Em

Pieces for Lesson 15

Danny Boy

Irish Traditional

Rit. or Ritard. means "gradual slowing down."

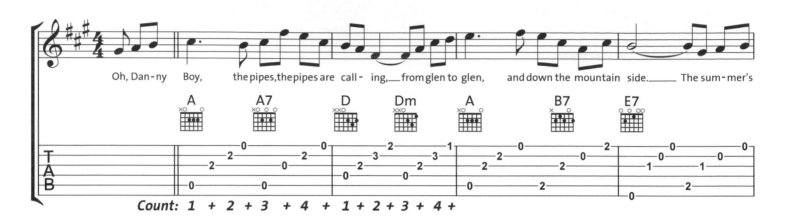

Oh, Dan-ny Boy, the pipes, the pipes are call-ing,___ from glen to glen, and down the mountain side.___ The sum-mer's

Count: 1 + 2 + 3 + 4 + 1 + 2 + 3 + 4 +

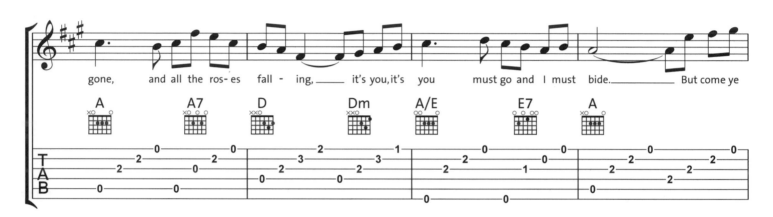

gone, and all the ros-es fall-ing,___ it's you, it's you must go and I must bide.___ But come ye

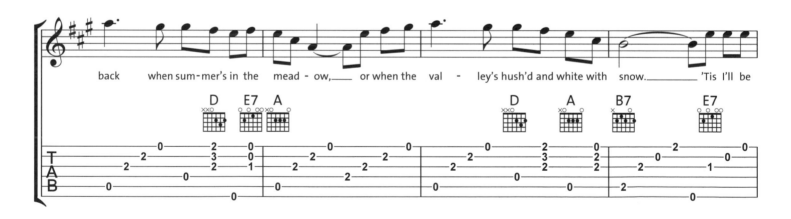

back when sum-mer's in the mead-ow,___ or when the val - ley's hush'd and white with snow.___ 'Tis I'll be

ritardando

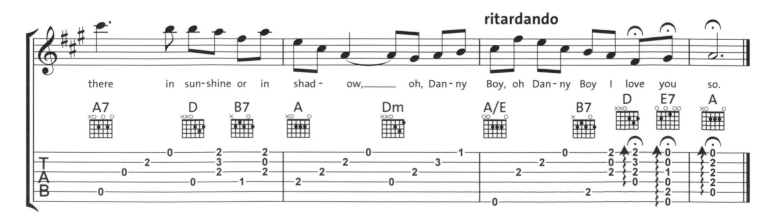

there in sun-shine or in shad-ow,___ oh, Dan-ny Boy, oh Dan-ny Boy I love you so.

test: *for* Lessons 11 to 15

1. Name the notes

Write the names of the following notes below each one.

(12)

2. Name the TAB notes

Write in the names of the following notes below each one.

(12)

3. Name the chords

Write the names of these chord symbols.

(10)

4. Fill in the blanks

Draw in the diagrams for the following chords.

B⁷   D   E

(6)

5. Alternate bass picking

Fill in the missing alternate bass notes for each chord where indicated (above each star).

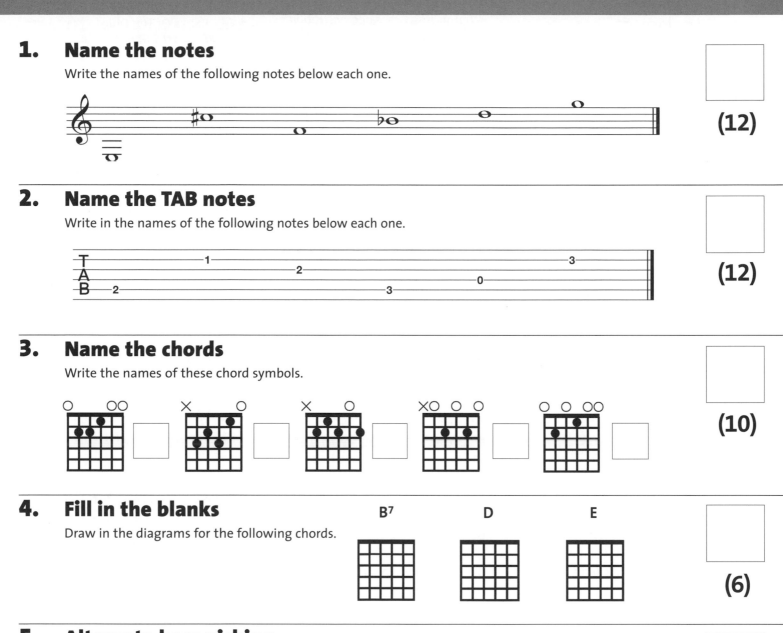

(10)

Total (50)

CD track listing

How to use the CD

After track 7, which gives an idea of how the guitar can sound, the backing tracks are listed in the order in which they appear in the book.

Look for the 💿 symbol in the book for the relevant demonstration or backing track.

3456789